FIVE-MINUTE MIRACLES

FIVE-MINUTE MIRACLES

373 Quick Daily Discoveries for You and Your Kids to Share

By Joni Hilton

RUNNING PRESS
PHILADELPHIA, PENNSYLVANIA

Canadian representatives: General Publishing Co., Ltd., 30 Lesmill Road, Don Mills, Ontario M3B 2T6.

International representatives: Worldwide Media Services, Inc., 30 Montgomery Street, Jersey City, New Jersey, 07302.

9 8 7 6 5 4 3 2 1
Digit on the right indicates the number of this printing.

ISBN 1–56138–140–3

Edited by Steven Zorn
Cover design by Nancy Loggins
Interior design by Nancy Loggins
Cover and interior illustrations by Matt Wawiorka

Typography: Gill Sans with Futura Bold, by
Richard Conklin, Philadelphia, Pennsylvania

This book may be ordered from the publisher.
Please add $2.50 for postage and handling.
But try your bookstore first!
Running Press Book Publishers
125 South Twenty-second Street
Philadelphia, Pennsylvania 19103

For Richie, Brandon,
Cassidy, and Nicole
(even if they did laugh when
my gingerbread house collapsed)

CONTENTS

R E A D Y !

"There never seems to be enough time!"

"Mornings are such a battle."

"Quality time takes too much quantity time."

"I wish we shared more intimate moments."

"Is there any way out from under the guilt?"

From the moment the alarm rings, most parents get caught up in a whirlwind of breakfast, backpacks, lunch boxes, day-care centers, homework assignments, school buses, car-pools, and their own daily work demands.

It doesn't seem to matter whether you're a single parent, a working mother, a househusband, or any other kind of mom or pop—everyone seems equally frazzled. Everyone wishes the family were more unified, more relaxed, more affectionate.

But I have the solution, believe it or not—and I stumbled upon it by accident! Usually, parents stumble upon trucks, dolls, and uniden-tifiable sections of formerly complete toys, but rarely do they happen upon a heck of a good idea. This was one of those times.

Somehow we finished breakfast early. Not very, very early, but about five minutes early. I had pulled out a lunch bag for my five-year-old, Richie. His brother, Brandon, three, sat beside him at our breakfast counter and suddenly recalled that today was a hot lunch day at school. Ah, so it is, I agreed. And then, noticing that we didn't need to hurry as we usually do, I smiled at my two little guys and said, "Hey, kids, watch this!" Then I blew up the paper bag and popped it. Well, they loved it.

The next morning, Richie and Brandon wanted another "surprise" after breakfast. Okay, I thought, my mind racing. I'll show you how to float a raw egg. (You dump lots of salt into the water.) *Ta-da!* They were enthralled.

Thus began our traditional "project time" for five minutes every day, right after breakfast.

It's made all the difference in how pleasantly our days begin, how close we feel as we laugh together, and how smart the boys are getting. This high point of our day has truly changed our lives.

Our mornings now go like clockwork, so we'll have plenty of time for "today's project." Amazingly, most of these projects take but five minutes, and many of them—like popping a bag—take just a few seconds.

It's pure fun, pure education, pure family time. My friends begged me to compile a calendar of suggestions so that they could begin their days the same way. So I've put together 12 months of projects, all inexpensive and all adaptable for a child of any age.

There are 31 suggestions for each month, even for the short month of February. Use them only on weekdays if you prefer, skip the ones that don't appeal to you, and let these projects prompt ideas of your own. Also included is a holiday bonus—plans for building a quick gingerbread house. You'll find it after December 31.

New concepts which promise to create stronger family bonds and brighter children usually need a few years of trial to be pronounced successful. Recently, I was fortunate to discover that a family I'd known and admired for years was already performing morning miracles. Their four children (all grown except for one teenager) had always impressed me as being very loving, close, and ready to laugh with their mom and dad. They didn't seem to feel the generation gap that parents dread as children grow up. Also, these kids were brilliant.

One of the daughters happened to mention to me that every morning before school, they'd gather around the table and play a game together. Just a standard game, like Scrabble or Boggle, but something that challenged their minds. They got smarter, and they also grew closer.

That may not be a scientific sampling, but it tells me that the concept works.

Now—get ready to perform a miracle.

S E T !

In this book you'll find more than a year's worth of five-minute project ideas. Every month includes these subjects:

art

cooking

drama

ethics/values

history

holidays/seasonal awareness

humor

imagination

language skills/reading

math

motor skills

music

physical activity

social studies

Longer projects.

You can do most of these activities in five minutes or less, but you may want to spend more time on a few of them. Projects that lend themselves to lazy weekends, or that can be split over two days, are marked with a clock symbol.

Seasonal projects.

Throughout the year are projects that relate to holiday celebrations. These projects are set off by a four-seasons symbol.

Food projects.

We do most of our daily discoveries in the morning. But some of the cooking projects (such as making soda floats) are better scheduled after school. You can easily adapt food-oriented projects to your own family's schedule and tastes. Cooking projects are denoted by a food symbol.

Series.

Throughout the year are several series which run for about a week, and which focus on one topic. These series are marked with a calendar symbol.

The topics are:

The American Frontier
Asia
Easter
Europe
Gift-making
Halloween
Independence Day
The Middle East
Latin America
Outer space
Polynesia
Thanksgiving

Here are some things I left out of this book:

Dissecting. Please. I am a wuss. No one is going to dissect so much as a gnat in my house. If you want to explore this area of science, be my guest; wonderful science-supply stores can provide you with everything you need for dissection. Maybe even the worms.

Excursions and field trips. There are so many truly wonderful places to explore with kids: you can tour a candy factory, a newspaper printing room, the post office, the fire department, a bakery, or a hospital. Plus there are zoos, concerts, theme parks, and other great outings. But these are more time-consuming.

Geographically limited ideas. Finding out how moist a cactus is inside or how a snowflake looks under a magnifying glass is exciting. But I've only included things that you can do *wherever* you live.

Magic. Maybe I'm just a klutz, but every time I've tried to master a trick—particularly those involving sleight-of-hand—I fluff it. Try them if you wish, but remember: lots of magic tricks are expensive. And to a child, nearly everything is already magic.

Origami. Intricate folding techniques and elaborate crafts simply take too much time to be included in this book. But they are wonderful and should be sought out and tried when you have a delicious chunk of time to invest.

Specific songs. Music is an important part of life, and I encourage you to sing often with your children, but in fairness to parents who can't read music, I decided not to print our favorite songs.

Sports and board games. Kids need both, but these activities take more time.

Story reading. This vital part of childhood should be given more than a "quick five" in the mornings. Because poems and stories are such a big part of our evenings, I've let other activities dominate the mornings.

Uncommon materials. We all happen upon the occasional great find (and you'll be amazed at how much thought you'll put into your trash before you throw it out, now that you'll be tuned into project ideas). But if the materials are not readily available to all—and for little or no money—I left them out.

G O !

• **Make sure you have the materials on hand.** Often, you don't need anything you don't already have around the house. But look a few days ahead, and be sure you have glue, a jar, string, and whatever else you might need.

• **Keep a separate project calendar.** After you read and understand the project, just a word or two written in a note to yourself will jog your memory. Transfer a month's worth of ideas you like onto your own calendar. Each morning (or better, the night before) look at the day's project to be sure you're all set. Some kids love the regimentation of a chart; let them help you make one to post upcoming projects.

• **Don't blame yourself if you miss a day.** Illnesses, erratic alarm clocks, and other unplanned events occasionally interrupt the schedule, so just remember: there's always tomorrow. It isn't the occasional setbacks that count; it's the basic, day-to-day lifestyle that's important. When holidays and vacations interrupt, remember that these are projects of a sort, too.

• **Laugh at the flops.** When our graham-cracker gingerbread house collapsed during construction, the kids fell off their chairs laughing. I played it up by pretending to be flabbergasted and outraged. When a clay we mixed stayed watery, I shouted into the bowl, "Hey! What's the big idea? You're supposed to get thick!" and the kids howled. Our disasters remain some of their favorite projects.

• **Supervise everything.** None of these projects is dangerous if done properly. But as you know, anything, from a shoebox to a cotton ball, can be dangerous.

• **Have the kids help with cleanup.** This will teach your children responsibility on top of whatever other subject they've just learned. It reinforces the idea of the whole family pitching in together, and it keeps mess-making to a minimum.

• **Adapt to the ages of your children.** When a project suggests learning numbers, why not teach Roman numerals to the older kids? If they can already write the alphabet, let them try calligraphy. There's always a way to scale it up, and in many cases I've suggested how at the end of the description.

• **Listen carefully, particularly during projects that involve some imagination or role-playing.** You'll be surprised at what you can learn about your child's worries and fears (or their strengths and blossoming virtues). You'll see puppets sharing, or maybe fighting. You'll hear stories about villains and heroes who turn out to be members of the family. Drama can open the door to help that might be needed. And it can reaffirm to you that your kids are adjusting to life beautifully.

As you listen, you'll see where interests and talents lie. One child may prefer art projects; another may like word games. You'll know where to encourage a talent, and where to work harder on a child's weaknesses.

• **Take pictures!** Instead of a scrapbook filled with the same smiling poses, why not capture the wide-eyed wonder of a child watching a homemade volcano? Or the silly grin of a child peeking out from behind a mask? These are projects that build intelligence and family closeness, but—let's admit it—they're priceless photo opportunities, too.

• **Don't worry that a project might be too advanced.** First of all, it won't be. For parents who can't fathom a two-year-old grasping the difference between a circle's radius and its diameter, just let me tell you that merely hearing the words "radius" and "diameter" makes a difference. When the child hears them later, the words won't be completely foreign. Just spending time together feels close, warm, and happy.

And remember—this isn't SuperKidism. There are no lectures or tests here—just playful laughter and dazzling discoveries.

1. **Play "I Love You More Than."** Spend a few minutes telling each other that "I love you more than pizza, sunsets, ice cream, my dog, dancing, rainbows, dinosaurs, cartoons, snowflakes," etc. Think of the things you love most. Talk about how wonderful it feels to be loved.

2. **Sculpt with aluminum foil.** Tear off a large piece, then tear it into smaller ones. Wrinkle and press it into bracelets, rings, monsters—anything you wish to sculpt.

3. **Button and unbutton.** For young kids, this is a good challenge. Older kids can race to see who can button and unbutton the fastest, using a stopwatch or timer. Older kids can also practice buttoning with their eyes closed, or with just one hand.

4. **Make graham-cracker fractions.** Break a cracker into halves and fourths. Talk about how many fourths it takes to make a

whole. Draw comparisons to a quarter of a dollar, and a quart being a fourth of a gallon. When you're through—what else?—eat the materials!

5. **Fact and friction.** Rub your hands together to demonstrate how friction creates heat. Older kids can learn about how friction also slows things down. (Imagine trying to run if you're waist-deep in water.) If you're mechanically inclined, show how the brakes on a bicycle rub to slow the bike. Explain that one of the tasks of a space scientist is to conquer the heat created by friction upon a fast-moving satellite as it zooms through the atmosphere.

6. **Make beanbags.** Fill an old sock with dried beans (lima, navy, any kind will do), and sew it closed. The best beanbags are not filled snugly to the seams; leave some space inside for the beans to shift. If you have time, color or decorate the sock with marking pens before you fill it with beans.

7. **Squeeze fresh orange juice.** Even without a juicer, you can make a delicious, high-energy drink. (Valencia oranges are best.) They'll yield more juice if you roll them on the kitchen counter, pressing with the palm of your hand.

Older kids can guess how many seeds will fall into the cup. You can also make orange-juice ice cubes, or mix the juice with soda water to make punch.

8. **Learn about roads.** Draw a road on a sheet of paper, and teach kids about the white and yellow lines. What do they mean where you live? Draw some road signs and discuss why we need them. Older kids can invent signs it would be good to have. How many signs are posted on your block?

9. **Take your pulse.** Press two fingers (not your thumbs) against the inside of your wrist until you can feel your pulse. Another good spot to try is against the side of your neck. Using a clock's second hand, measure your heart rate. Time your pulse for 15 seconds, then multiply by four. Smaller kids can learn where their heart is. Now run in place and take your pulse again. When we do more work, the heart pumps harder to carry more oxygen from our lungs.

10. **"Keep It Up!"** Blow up some balloons and toss them in the air. Try to keep them aloft for as long as possible. Older kids can use more balloons and dash around as they try to keep each one from falling.

11. **Paint with glue.** I do this one outdoors, but it can also be done inside on newspaper. First squirt white glue onto a sheet of construction paper, in any design you choose. Now sprinkle sawdust, glitter, sand, confetti, pencil shavings, even shredded pages from magazines, onto the glue. Shake the excess "glitter" into the wastebasket. Kids are always delighted with their creations and love to see their artwork displayed in the home.

12. **Solid to liquid to gas.** Demonstrate the various forms of water. Start by melting some ice in a saucepan. After it turns to liquid, boil it until you get steam. This shows the three forms of water: ice (solid), water (liquid), and steam (gas). You can also point out that the hottest part of the steam is actually the invisible water vapor closest to the saucepan. When the steam turns into a white mist, the vapor is cooling and forming tiny water droplets.

13. **Trace your child's hand.** On a blank sheet of paper, outline your child's hand with a pen or pencil. When he lifts his hand, encourage him to draw a miniature "world" there. He can make something different in each finger—his thumb can become a lake, his pinky a desert. Older kids can transform their hands into elaborate cities.

14. **Tie your shoelaces.** Younger kids will love the feeling of independence that this brings, and older kids can try it with their eyes closed. Or, they can lace their shoes with the bow at the toe end. (The shoes are harder to remove, but the look is  unique.) Try lacing each shoe with two shoelaces in wild colors!

15. **Write a storybook.** Invite your kids to tell a story. You can be the scribe while they work on the illustrations. Kids will want to read those very special "books" again and again.

16. **Study the surface tension of water.** Fill a glass with water, then add several more spoonfuls. You'll see how the water "mounds" over the rim of the glass. Surface tension makes water seem as if a clear, flexible film is covering its surface. This is because water molecules are attracted to each other and stick together. The molecules  on top are being pulled down by the ones below. This same

property causes raindrops to be shaped like droplets and allows water-strider bugs to walk on the surface of ponds.

Try floating a paper clip, a needle, or a staple on the surface of the water. It'll work if you keep the object flat and slide it gently onto the surface, starting from the edge of the glass.

17. **Make papier-mâché banks or vases.** Tear newspaper into small pieces, then dip them into a bowl containing equal parts white glue and water. Now wrap the wet pieces of newspaper around an empty tin can, or any other container. Let the creations dry on a sheet of waxed paper. Later you can paint or decorate them as you wish

We used a can with a plastic cover to create a piggy bank. First we cut a slit in the cover and then we glued a fat cork onto it to make the piggy's nose. Four smaller corks became the legs. A pipe cleaner (wrapped first around a pencil to make it curly) became the tail.

18. **Create carpet drawings.** Using yarn or string, you can "draw" pictures on the carpet. (If your home isn't carpeted, simply spread out a rug, towel, or blanket.) Give your child a length of

string, and show her how to dangle it onto the surface to form a design. You can easily alter the picture or erase it completely by pulling the string!

19. **Cut paper snowflakes.** First, you'll need to make a square sheet of white paper. Take a standard sheet of typing paper, and fold the upper-right corner down to the left edge of the sheet. Now crease the fold. You'll notice a few inches of

extra paper along the bottom. Cut this off. Now unfold the paper and you have a square. To make snowflakes, fold it back again, corner to corner, forming a triangle. Continue to fold corner to corner, twice more. Use safety scissors to cut small holes and diamonds through all layers of paper. Now open it up and "ooh" and "ahh" over the pretty results. Discuss how no two snowflakes are alike. You can hang the lacy masterpieces in the window to celebrate winter.

20. **What's it weigh?** Select books, bowls, and toys, and guess which objects are the heaviest. Then test your guesses using a kitchen or bathroom scale. Even older kids will have a

tough time guessing, as looks can truly be deceiving. Have them weigh themselves, too.

You can also fill a bucket with water to show how heavy water is.

21. **Switch roles.** Today the kids will be the grownups, and the grownups will be the kids. Aren't you glad this lasts only five minutes? Kids will love being "the boss," and you'll be amazed at some of the things they'll say in an effort to sound like you.

Older kids may even have the chance to experience some of the responsibilities involved in parenting. If you say something like, "I don't think I'll go to school today," or "I think I'll just eat candy today," your "parent" will have to decide what's permissible.

22. **Make soap!** Or rather, re-make soap. Melt chips of hand soap in a saucepan containing a little water. When the soap is soft enough to be molded (but cool enough not to burn you), press the mixture into cookie cutters. Or, resculpt it with your hands into shapes. These soaps make wonderful gifts.

23. **"Sew What?"** Using a scrap of fabric and a blunt needle, help a child to make even stitches. (Sometimes younger children like to work on a piece of burlap, or a loosely woven canvas.)

Older kids can cross-stitch, embroider their own shirts, or monogram a sweatshirt.

24. **Make beautiful scribbles together.** Take a black crayon and scribble on a blank sheet of paper. Make sure the scribble has lots of large loops and open spaces, rather than solid masses of black. Next use brightly colored crayons and completely fill each space with a different color. The results will be as pretty as stained glass!

25. **Discover a new country.** Select a spot on the globe or on a world map, where there is no land. Then draw a small "country" on a piece of paper. Cut it out, and tape it to the globe. Ask your child to name the new country and describe the weather, vegetation, people, and customs. He can even plan a pretend vacation there.

Ask older kids to tell you about how the country is governed or what its problems are and how they're solved. Tell a joke that gets big laughs in this new country.

26. **Learn about colors.** Cut apart paint chips from a hardware store, or make your own chips with colored paper, and mix them in a bowl. Have your child remove the chips one by one, and

arrange them from darkest to lightest. Talk about pastels, and how you add white to lighten a color, black to darken it.

Older kids can decide which green is yellowest, and which is bluest. Which red seems more orange and which is most purple?

27. **Read maps.** Using any road map, locate rivers, highways, and borders. In discovery number eight this month, you learned about roads; now see how they are indicated on a map. If you have a map of your city, observe the city's shape. Does it look different from how your child pictured it?

28. **Keep your eye on the sky.** Discuss how clouds are formed by tiny droplets of water, or ice crystals, and learn their names: cirrus (the wispy white clouds), cumulus (the puffy white clouds), stratus (the horizontally layered clouds) and nimbus (the dark storm clouds). Explain that many clouds are a combination of these four types.

Look outside: What kinds of clouds are in the sky today? Do any of the clouds form recognizable shapes? Older kids can make cloud charts and record the kinds of clouds they see in the sky each day.

29. **Make a flip movie.** These are a blast. Draw a face in the upper right-hand corner of each card in a stack of 3x5 cards. Make the eyes roll, the tongue stick out, or a beard grow by changing the drawing a *tiny* bit on each succeeding card. You can draw a bud opening, a balloon popping, or just get a simple dot to dance around. Now staple the stack on the left side, being careful to keep the cards in order. Flip quickly through them and your drawings will actually appear to move. Explain that this is how real cartoon movies are made. Encourage your child to make sound effects as she flips through the booklet.

30. **Make music.** Blow into a narrow-necked, empty bottle or jar to make a windy, flutelike sound. Notice how the sound changes when you add a little water. Horns were once made from shells, bamboo, and animal horns. Older kids can try to create varying pitches and even play a tune!

31. **Whip up indoor snow sculptures.** This is a real favorite. In a mixing bowl, beat soap flakes (baby detergent works best) with

a little water. Try just a few drops of water at first, as even a half-cup of soap will whip up a big lather. When the lather gets stiff, let your kids sculpt snowmen, igloos, make handprints—whatever. I like working with soap even better than using clay; when you're finished, the kids' hands are guaranteed to be clean!

1. **Draw with your toes.** Holding a pen or crayon between your toes, draw or write on a piece of paper. If this doesn't get you giggling, nothing will!

2. **Test your memory.** Place five to ten small objects (fewer if your child is young; more if he's older) on a pie tin or plate. Give him a few seconds to study the items, then have him close his eyes while you remove one of the items. Now tell him to open his eyes and try to guess which item you took away. Kids enjoy this game at parties, too.

3. **Create a vacuum.** I did this for my kindergartner's class and received a standing ovation. Here's how you do it: First, you'll need an empty, one-gallon *glass* bottle with a narrow neck (cranberry juice is sold in these) and a peeled hard-boiled egg. The neck of the bottle should be slightly narrower than the egg. Now place torn newspapers inside the bottle and light the papers with a long

match. Quickly place the egg over the bottle neck. Because the fire is rapidly drawing in oxygen, a strong vacuum will be created in the bottle and the egg will be sucked in with a loud *thunk!*

Make sure to put out the fire and dispose of the bottle.

4. **Make a winter butterfly.** Using tiny chips of crayon, you can create a beautiful picture. Sprinkle the chips into a folded sheet of paper. Now, keeping the crayons folded *inside*, iron the paper. The heat from the iron will melt the chips, and when you unfold the paper you'll have a gorgeous winter butterfly!

5. **Draw different types of homes.** Explain that children around the world live in different types of homes, and see how many kinds of dwellings your child can think of. Did she name tepee, igloo, tent, house, apartment, hut, boat?

6. **Have a hand-shadow show.** Shine a flashlight on the wall of a darkened room, and create as many creatures as you can. Link your thumbs and flap your straight fingers to make a bird. Use one hand for the mouth and the other hand to make the antlers of a deer. Spread fingers out and

wiggle them to form a spider. Hold two fingers up to become the ears
of a rabbit and "hop" across the wall.

7. **Concoct "sky's-the-limit" sandwiches.**
Kids rarely have the chance to do something
with no restrictions. Today let them make
sandwiches with whatever ingredients they
like and see how creative they can be. (One
of my kids made a ham, peanut-butter,
cheese, and fruit-roll sandwich, using two
cookies for the bread.)

8. **Search for shapes.** See who can find the most shapes
around the house. Have your children search for a circle, square,
triangle, and rectangle. Can they find an oval or diamond? Older

kids can race to see who can be first to find
these shapes—or look for more complex
figures such as a hexagon or a parallelogram.

9. **Make traditional valentines.** Cut hearts
of various sizes from red, pink, and white
construction paper. Add lace doilies, stickers,
glitter, and ribbons, if you like.

10. **Learn odd and even numbers.** Take turns shouting out a number while the others decide if it's odd or even. You can show younger kids which numbers are odd and which are even by drawing a line of numbers on a piece of paper, and having them circle every other one. For older kids who already know odd and even, you can play this factor game: Pick a number such as three, five, or six, and then whenever you shout a larger number such as 12, 15, or 24 they must shout "yes" or "no" in response to whether it's divisible by the smaller number you selected.

11. **Play with sponges.** Purchase a real sponge from a beauty supply store, or just use one from the supermarket, and watch how it soaks up water. Wring it out afterward and measure how much water was soaked up. Scientists used to think sponges were plants, but since sponges have to eat food—and don't manufacture their own—now it's believed that they are animals. Their skeletons hold a surprising amount of water. Most live on the bottom of warm oceans, but some live in fresh water and lakes, too. There are about 5,000 species of sponges, some more than four feet wide!

12. **Draw pennies.** Celebrate Abraham Lincoln's birthday by sketching pennies. As the kids draw,

point out the tiny image of Lincoln in the impression of the Memorial on the back of the penny and tell them the legend about Lincoln's extraordinary honesty: One day when he was working as a clerk in a store, a woman overpaid by one cent. Lincoln chased after her for a long way, just to return the penny.

You can also tell kids about his other achievements, such as his role in abolishing slavery in the United States. Older kids can try to sketch an exact replica of a penny from memory.

13. **Learn about animals.** Have your child draw or name an animal that has whiskers. Now name one that has fins. Next try one with a tail, hooves, claws, feathers, and spots. Older kids can limit their guesses to farm animals, or zoo animals, or animals whose names begin with certain letters.

14. **Make love bloom.** Cut out tiny hearts from pink construction paper (or use heart stickers) and set them aside. Have your child draw a stem on a piece of paper, then glue the tiny pink hearts onto the top, to form flower petals. Older kids can make their bouquets more elaborate, by adding more stems and more intricate petals. These flowers can become a charming valentine.

15. **Make your own paper plates.** Take a heavy piece of

paper and fold it down one inch on all sides. Staple the corners. Now you can eat breakfast on your homemade plates!

 16. **Make a cherry tree.** Draw a tree trunk on a sheet of paper; set it aside. Cut out small leaves and cherries from green and red construction paper. While your child glues them onto the tree, tell her the fable about George Washington saying, "I cannot tell a lie," when he chopped down his father's cherry tree. Explain that this American folk tale sprang from admiration for a man who was already known for his great honesty and integrity. Two more false stories about our first president are that he had wooden teeth, and that he threw a dollar across the Potomac River.

17. **Create string-and-ink designs.** Dip a thin string into ink or paint, then twirl it onto the right or left half of a sheet of construction paper. Fold the other half of the paper over the string, and press down as you slowly remove the string. Now open the paper to reveal the lovely painting inside!

18. **Learn about advertising.** All children pass billboards, watch TV commercials, and see ads in magazines and newspapers. Explain that advertising is a device used for selling products, and have your child invent a commercial to sell a favorite toy. Older kids can clip

magazine ads and discuss them with you. Encourage them to question some of the ads' messages, such as, "Use this aftershave and women will adore you," or "If you don't put this snack in your child's lunch box, she won't be popular." Kids will love learning about this side of advertising, and they'll become more savvy consumers in the process.

19. **It's eggs-asperating!** Try to break a raw egg by squeezing it in the palm of one hand. You won't be able to break it. (It's best to do this one over the sink—just in case.) Unlike cracking an egg by hitting it on the side, your hand spreads the pressure over the entire surface of the egg. The egg's shape is extremely strong under pressure. That's why architects like to design buildings with arches and domes.

20. **Make a family tree.** Create a chart of your family's genealogy on poster board. If you have photos, glue them into place. Talk about the importance of family. Tell stories about your grandparents or other relatives.

 Begin a six-day series on Latin America. Tell your children that our neighbors to the south include Mexico, Central and South America.

21. **Make a poncho.** Cut a horizontal slit in the center of an old towel or a yard of fabric. If you don't have any fabric, simply use a large sheet of newspaper. Now make the slit into a T-shape by cutting a smaller slit perpendicular to the large one (this forms a sort of V-neck). Slip the towel over your head, and you have a poncho! Let your kids paint or color it brightly to look more authentic. Real ones are made from wool blankets and are worn mostly by villagers in the cold mountain areas.

22. **Learn about parrots.** Help your child draw a parrot on a sheet of paper. Then glue on some bright feathers. (These can be purchased at a craft store, or simply made from pieces of colored construction paper.) Discuss how these birds mimic songs and words. Ask your child to name other animals that live in Latin America. (Hints: exotic butterflies, monkeys, birds, lizards, snakes, and crocodiles.)

23. **Make maracas.** These are also called "shakers" and they make wonderful musical instruments. To make one, papier-mâché a small, inflated balloon, just as you did the can in January's discovery number 17. Make

sure to leave uncovered the area where the mouth of the balloon is tied. In a day or two, after the papier-mâché has dried, pop the balloon. (The papier-mâché will retain its oval shape.) Pull out the balloon, pour in a few beans or some dry rice, and patch over the opening with more papier-mâché or tape. Paint or color it, and get ready to make music!

A faster alternative is to put the beans in a can with a secure lid.

24. **Carry things on your head.** Explain to your kids that many people in Latin America (and the rest of the world) use this method to carry baskets of cloth or food, purchases from markets, and jugs of water. Borrow books about Latin America from the library ahead of time, to show kids pictures of how this is done. Now let your kids try carrying household items on their heads—nonbreakables, of course!

25. **Make tortillas.** Using just water and dry cornmeal, you can make tortillas, a staple of Mexican cooking. Experiment with the proportions until you can work up a fairly stiff dough. Pat the mixture into a thin disk. Now heat some oil in a frying pan, and fry the tortillas. Sometimes they turn out like pita bread, which you can use for sandwiches, and other times, they come out like crispy chips, which you can melt cheese over, to make nachos. Either

way, they're a real treat!

26. **Break open a coconut.** Coconuts grow in tropical areas of the world.

I do this one outside because I like to use a sledgehammer! But before you crack the coconut, drive a screwdriver or nail into the dimples to drain the milk. Let your kids sample it, along with chunks of the white meat. (A Guatemalan woman once gave me this tip: When you're choosing a coconut, shake it first. If you can't hear any liquid sloshing around inside, the coconut has dried out. Choose another!)

This concludes the Latin America series.

27. **What's it worth?** Even very young kids can learn to tell the difference between a dime, a penny, and other coins. Older kids can add up the value of several different coins, or practice making change.

28. **Make faces.** Draw 10 to 15 faces ahead of time, three or four to a page. Fill in only the nose and eyes, making sure they're all identical. Now let your child add the mouth and eyebrows to a few. Notice the wide variety of emotions these characters seem to have, just from different mouths and eyebrows. See if your kids can

make one face look angry, one afraid, one surprised, and one happy.

29. **News about newspapers.** Show kids a newspaper and point out the headlines in large, dark type and the captions in small type under photos. Explain the sections of the paper, such as world news, local news, sports, arts and entertainment, and business. For older kids, read some headlines aloud and see if they're able to guess which section they're from.

30. **Make a crown.** Cut a lengthwise zigzag down the middle of a sheet of construction paper. Then staple the two halves together at each end to form a crown. Your child can decorate the crown with artwork, numbers, or letters.

 31. **Scramble some green eggs and ham.** Inspired by Dr. Seuss, I've found that you can actually eat green eggs and ham! Eggs take food coloring amazingly well, and you can make them green—or any other color your kids request. Scramble them in the frying pan and enjoy a colorful breakfast!

1. **Search for spring.** Walk outside and look for traces of new life. Find tiny buds. Unwrap one and look at the layers. (If you live in a colder region, you may need to wait another month to do this.)

2. **Make rainbow popsicles.** The night before you do this discovery, pour about one inch of papaya, apple, or peach juice into several small paper cups or popsicle forms. Put them in the freezer. In the morning let kids place popsicle sticks in the cups, then add another inch of juice, this time using a different color, such as grape or cranberry. Return the pops to the freezer. By that afternoon you'll have a perfect after-school snack. (You can easily add another layer—try pink lemonade, pink guava, or orange juice.)

3. **Learn about static electricity.** Demonstrate a negative electrical charge by rubbing an inflated balloon on someone's hair. As you do this, tiny particles called electrons move from the hair to the balloon, electrically charging both. Notice how the balloon

will stick to a wall. This is because the charged balloon attracts the uncharged wall. See what other things will be attracted to this negatively charged balloon. Will it pick up bits of thread or paper?

4. **Create a parachute.** Tie a knot in each corner of a handkerchief or scarf. Toss it into the air and watch it float down. (We started out by tying small rocks into the corners and dropping them off our balcony. They fell like . . . well, like rocks. So our experiment didn't work very well. But the kids roared and had a heck of a good time anyway.)

5. **Which freezes first?** You say cold water freezes first because it's already halfway there? Ha! I say hot! In small quantities, hot water really does freeze faster because of evaporation.

Pour a small amount of boiling water into a cup, and an equal amount of cold into another cup. (Use just a little bit—remember, these are five-minute projects.) Now wait a minute or two, then check the results.

6. **Make a paper clothes line.** Draw a clothes line on a sheet of paper. Now cut tiny shirts, socks, and pants out of scraps of fabric, and glue them on. Discuss how people all over the world dry their clothes this way, mentioning that it saves lots of energy

and can be very efficient, especially on a windy March day!

7. **Practice writing your name.** Show younger kids how to print their names while older kids write theirs in cursive. They can even turn the paper sideways and color in the loops and swirls.

8. **Play "Simon Says."** Kids have been enjoying this game for generations. To refresh your memory about the rules, here's how it's played: First, select one person to be Simon. His job is to tell the others what to do, prefacing his commands with "Simon Says." (For example, "Simon says, sit down," or "Simon says, pat your head.") Then Simon throws a curve: He gives an order without first saying "Simon Says." If you aren't paying attention and do it anyway, you lose. Now *you* must be Simon and try to catch the others.

9. **Make a terrarium.** A terrarium usually contains plants and animals (such as worms or insects), which exchange oxygen and carbon dioxide. But you can also make one containing only plants.

Here's how to do it: Use a clean jar, bottle, or a glass bowl. Spread a thick layer of pebbles on the bottom for drainage. Cover it with soil and tiny plants. Now arrange colored shells, driftwood, interesting rocks, aquarium gravel, even tiny figurines inside. Your terrarium will make a great gift.

10. **Experiment with magnets.** Find out what magnets will stick to. Try the refrigerator, and wood, brass, and copper surfaces. Will your magnets stick to the doorknobs? See if you can attract paper clips or pins.

11. **Look at the engine of a car.** Learn the name of at least one part. Older kids can name more parts, and may want to research how an engine works.

 12. **Make shamrocks.** Get ready for St. Patrick's Day by cutting shamrocks out of green construction paper. To pay tribute to the "In like a lion, out like a lamb" month of March, draw faces on your shamrocks, to resemble lions with a mane, and sheep with fleece. Display them on a wall or window.

13. **Learn about levers.** Show that you can lift heavy objects as long as there is a stationery place to rest the lever. Rest a ruler on a spool, or a tube (the fulcrum). Place a book (the resistance) on the "down" side of the ruler. Now press your hand (the force) on the top end, and you can lift the book! If the lever is long enough, you can lift the book with one finger!

14. **Make pompon flowers.** Weave a 3-foot strand of yarn over and under the tines of a fork. Now thread a shorter piece of yarn (or a twist-tie) under the yarn in the middle space of the tines. Pull this shorter piece up, forcing the loops off the fork, and tie it in the middle. Make a tight knot. You now have a tiny

pompon. Older kids can sew these onto sweaters and socks. Try fastening them to pipe cleaners to create a spring bouquet.

 Easter often falls during March, but swap the projects in this seven-day Easter series with next month's activities if Easter comes in April this year. Non-Christians can celebrate the springtime element of each project.

15. **Make bunny puppets.** Hold a paper bag upside-down so that you can put your hand up inside it. The flap at the top (which usually becomes the bottom of the bag) will serve as the bunny's face. Cut out of colored construction paper: two bunny ears, two eyes, a little pink nose, and some whiskers (which can be made of yarn or pipe cleaners). Glue these onto the face part. Next cut out

a pink oval for the tummy. A cotton ball glued on to the back of the bag becomes the tail and completes the puppet.

16. **Blow eggs.** Make a tiny hole in an uncooked egg and a slightly larger hole at the opposite end. (I use a pin.) Blow into the tiny hole and the raw egg will come out the larger hole. Use the raw egg for scrambled eggs, and set aside the shells for tomorrow.

17. **Decorate the eggs.** Cover the eggs you blew yesterday with rhinestones and glitter. Felt-tip markers also work well.

18. **Create lace Easter eggs.** Blow up and knot some small balloons. Dip lengths of lightweight string into liquid starch found near laundry detergents in the grocery store. (Yarn stores sell thin, multicolored string that works great.) Coat the balloons with pretty swirls of string, covering most of their surface. Let the balloons dry on waxed paper. Tonight pop the balloons. The dry string will stay stiff, in the beautiful, swirly designs you made. Pull the balloons out and display the eggs. These are real dazzlers, and make nice gifts, or unusual fillers for Easter baskets.

19. **Make egg-shaped pancakes.** Let your children decorate the pancakes with sprinkles or chocolate chips.

20. **Here comes Peter Cottontail.** Buy or draw a simple outline of a bunny. Let younger kids glue cotton balls onto it to make him fluffy. Older kids can use just cotton balls and glue to form a three-dimensional rabbit.

21. **Decorate a bunny cake.** The night before you do this project, purchase or make one round cake and white frosting. Today cut the cake in half and stand the two pieces side by side,

with the rounded sides up. Next frost the cake white, so it resembles the bunny's crouched body. Place the cake on a bed of "grass," which I make by shaking up some shredded coconut and green food coloring in a jar.

Have your kids help to decorate the cake by cutting two paper ears out of construction paper and inserting them into one end. They can use a red gumdrop for the nose and two pink jellybeans for the eyes. Shoestring licorice works well for whiskers, and a Hostess-brand "snowball" cupcake is perfect for the tail.

This cake delights kids and can be frosted and decorated within five minutes, as long as you start with the baked cake and have all the other materials ready.

This concludes the Easter series.

22. **Be an egg detective.** How do you tell a boiled egg from a raw one? Spin them, stop them, and let go. The inertia of the liquid in the raw egg will keep it spinning longer.

23. **Make a rainbow.** Kids can paint a rainbow with watercolors (or using bits of colored paper). Older kids can try to paint their rainbows so that the colors blend into one another, as they do in a real rainbow. (Tip: Use lots of water.) By the way, to remember the order of colors in the rainbow, think of Roy G. Biv—the letters in his name are the first letters of the colors of the rainbow: Red, Orange, Yellow, Green, Blue, Indigo, Violet.

24. **Find things around the house that start with certain letters.** If this is too difficult for young kids, have them look for things that begin with the *ba* or *ga* sound. Older kids can look for objects that rhyme with certain words. For example, have them search for something that rhymes with "more." You can keep scaling it up: "I see something that has seven letters in it," and so on.

25. **Get a lift.** Point a blow-dryer upward, and turn it on. (Do this *for* your kids and have them *watch*.) Now ask the kids to hold a Ping-Pong ball over the dryer, and watch it rise in the air stream. (You can demonstrate the same principle with a small scrap of paper.) This is one of my kids' all-time favorites.

 26. **Make paint or dye from plants.** Gather leaves and flowers of various colors. Add a drop of water and then mash them with a mortar and pestle (or use a bowl and the back of a spoon, or a pie tin and a rock). Save the dye in small jars, or pour it onto an old shirt to see if the dye will color it. Explain that this is how people actually used to dye wool and make colored cloth.

 27. **Tie-dye clothing.** Using the dye you made (or packaged dye from the store), tie-dye a T-shirt. It's so easy, you won't believe it.

Just wad up a shirt in several places and hold the wads in place with rubber bands. Now dip part of each of the "tied" sections of the shirt into the dye and hold it there for a few seconds. When you're through, rinse the dyed sections in the sink and take off the rubber bands. *Voilà!* You've just designed a new shirt.

When we do this, we always spread out plenty of newspapers and use large buckets of Rit-brand dye. Be sure to wear old clothes or smocks, as the dye is permanent.

28. **Make a puzzle.** Cut into uneven pieces a magazine page your child has selected and let her try to put it back together again. Older kids can do the cutting themselves, and cut more pieces. Another variation is to paste the page onto stiff cardboard before you cut, so that the puzzle can be used repeatedly. Or turn the pieces over and put together the unknown picture on back.

29. **Make flowers from tissues.** First tear two facial tissues in half lengthwise. (Use different colors, if you have them.) Separate  the two-ply layers in all four pieces, so that you have eight sheets. Stack them evenly, one on top of another. Now, accordion-fold the stack from end to end. When you complete the fan, tie it around the middle with a pipe cleaner, a twist-tie, or a rubber band. (Pipe cleaners are best, as they can form the flower's stem as well.) Separate each layer of tissue from the others, pulling it towards the pipe cleaner. As you

do this on each side, a beautiful flower will begin to bloom.

30. **See sound.** Put a few grains of dry rice on top of a drum or an empty oatmeal box with a lid. As you lightly beat the drum, show your child how the rice "dances." Explain that this vibrating is the same way sound travels, radiating and bumping air molecules. Dropping a pebble into water and then watching the ripples illustrates the same principle.

31. **Try to freeze salt water.** Explain to your kids that salt water resists freezing, and then demonstrate this principle. Fill one shallow ice-cube tray with salt water and one with fresh water. (Make sure it's only a small amount of water—this experiment has to work in five minutes.) Put the trays in the freezer. In five minutes compare the two trays. The salt water will be slushy, but not frozen solid.

1. **Play April Fools' jokes.** Try one of the classics—switching salt with sugar, oiling a doorknob—or make up one of your own. Kids love playing verbal tricks like, "Hey! You have ketchup on your shirt!" and then squealing, "April Fools'!"

2. **Grow sugar crystals.** It will be several days before you actually observe these tiny crystals starting to form, but you can begin to set up this project today.

Bring one cup of water to a boil. Remove it from the burner, and add one to two cups of sugar, stirring until it's completely dissolved. Explain to your kids that the sugar is now broken up into tiny molecules that you can't even see. Pour this solution into a clear glass. Now tie a piece of string to a stick or a pencil, and rub the string with dry sugar. Immerse the dangling string into the glass of water and let the pencil or stick rest on the top of the glass. Be careful not to disturb it. In a few days you'll see clear crystals of sugar forming on the string. If you wish, eat this rock candy.

3. **Guess the songs.** Hum a tune your child knows, and see if he can guess its name. Older kids can be given just one or two opening notes. Vary the game by beating out the rhythm, or having the child think of a tune while *you* try to guess its name.

4. **Learn math columns.** Fold a blank sheet of paper into four lengthwise columns. Use this paper to teach "here is the ones column, here is the tens column." Show that 14 is one mark in the tens column and four marks in the ones column. And so on. Say a number and see if your child can make the appropriate marks.

5. **Make tiny tops.** Slice a carrot crosswise one-half to one-inch thick, and stick a toothpick through each slice. Now twirl the tops on a counter or floor and watch them spin!

6. **Grow a carrot.** Cut a carrot in half crosswise, leaving the greenery on top. Stand the top half in a small dish and hold it in place with pebbles. Cover the pebbles with water. Pretty, feathery leaves will grow from the top in a few days.

7. **What is it?** Place an assortment of objects in a heavy sock or bag. (Good items are a tennis ball, hair curler, screw, emery board, button, and toy car.) Now blindfold your child and have her reach

into the sock and feel the items, guessing what each one is. For older kids, make the game harder by using coins, measuring spoons, and other less distinct objects.

8. **Pretend to be a seed.** Play music if you like, and then crouch so that you're very tiny. Slowly unfold as you grow, stretching into a lovely bloom.

Explain to your kids that seeds need soil, warmth, and water to grow. Ask your child what kind of plant or flower she is. What color is she? Do bees like her? Does she grow in the sun or shade?

9. **Discuss growing up.** Kids love monitoring how grown up they're becoming. Draw pictures of things your young child *used* to use, such as a crib, a bottle, and a diaper. Then talk about the things he will use one day: car keys, a computer, a checkbook, and an iron. Encourage your child to talk about the differences between being a baby and being his present age. What changes does he anticipate as he grows up?

Older kids can write a poem about the differences between things babies and adults use. Or they can try forming as many words as they can out of the letters in longer words such as "highchair," or "babysitter." (Let them think of other words to work with.)

10. **Make caterpillars.** Take an empty cardboard egg carton and discard the lid. Then cut the carton in half lengthwise. Invert the egg carton so that the hollow side is down. (These bumps will form the lumpy backs of two caterpillars.)

Your child can use markers or watercolors to decorate the caterpillars in bright spring colors. You can form the antennae on one end by punching two holes and inserting short sections of pipe cleaners or twist-ties.

11. **Learn to braid.** Tie three pieces of string or yarn together at one end and show your kids how to braid them. Older kids can get fancy, and make three braids—then braid *those* together.

12. **Draw an underwater scene.** Encourage kids to imagine an underwater story and draw a scene from it. They may want to include a pirate's treasure chest.

With older kids, you can talk about the lost city of Atlantis or the sinking of the *Titanic*. Discuss oceanography, and ways to harness the ocean's energy.

13. **Shine pennies.** Dip some pennies in a solution of one-half cup of vinegar and four tablespoons of salt. (Or use ketchup; it works, too!)

14. **Have a hugging contest.** Today, see who can give the best hugs. Our family does this all the time, and have for years. It brings more joy into our home than any other project.

15. **Make a kazoo.** Save a cardboard tube, such as the one inside a roll of paper towels or toilet paper. Now cut a circle of waxed paper (about five inches in diameter) and wrap it over one end of the tube. Secure it with a rubber band. Hum into the tube and you can play any song you like!

Begin a seven-day series on Asia. Show your child the Far East on a map, and tell·her that Asia has more than ·40 countries. It's the largest continent, and has the most people living there.

16. **Fold a fan.** Explain to your child that folded fans originated in Japan, around A.D. 700. They are often used in ceremonial dances. Here's how to make your own: Draw a pretty picture on a sheet of paper, and fold it back and forth so that it becomes pleated like

an accordion. Each pleat should be about a half-inch wide. Staple one end together, which becomes the part your child holds. Now take turns fanning one another with your creation.

17. **Make a mosaic.** First spread out some newspaper to make cleanup easier. Now pencil-sketch a simple drawing or design on a sheet of paper. Spread glue in one section of the drawing, then sprinkle on some rice, beans, seeds, or noodles. Shake off the excess, and discard. Spread glue in another section of your drawing, and this time, sprinkle on a new color or texture. Repeat the process until the mosaic is filled in.

Explain to your kids that Asian artists make elaborate mosaics using these items, painstakingly placing each tiny detail with a pair of tweezers.

18. **Practice flower arranging.** Japanese flower arrangements stand out for their simple elegance and ability to direct the eye. If you didn't have time to research this topic, you can still appreciate the beauty of nature's blooms and arrange a bouquet that's pleasing to your child. Encourage your child to vary the heights and the kinds of blossoms. Don't forget to include some greenery.

19. **Eat breakfast with chopsticks.** Cereal can be a fun

challenge (but no fair sticking a chopstick through a Cheerio). For more authentic flavor, use rice you've prepared the night before, or the kind that cooks in one minute, sprinkled with some soy sauce. Serve it in bowls and eat at a low table if you like, sitting on the floor. This is one time when you *want* your rice to come out sticky!

20. **Become a Chinese dragon.** In China, the dragon symbolizes wealth and good luck. New Year's parades include a colorful dragon to keep evil spirits away. Throw a blanket over your heads and weave through the house. Kids love being hidden under a blanket, and they'll have fun leading you through surprise twists and turns. Chinese music can provide a nice background. You can be a Chinese dragon with only two people, but the more the merrier!

21. **Kick up your heels!** Today, try some high kicks like they use in Korean karate. China, Japan, and Okinawa have styles of karate, too, but Korea's *tae kwon do* emphasizes kicking. Have your child kick into the air, and measure how high he can kick. Just as real karate students can earn yellow belts, purple belts, and so on, perhaps you could make up your own system of awarding colored belts.

22. **Make a Japanese watercolor painting.** Ahead of time,

borrow a book about Japanese art from the library and show kids some samples of watercolors. Now create your own: Dilute some paints for a misty, soft effect, and use delicate strokes while painting a crane, a mountain, a boat, a tree, or some blossoms. Older kids can try calligraphy.

This concludes the Asia series.

23. **Guess rhymes.** Read poetry aloud with your kids and let them guess the next word in the verse. Start with familiar nursery rhymes such as, "Mary had a little lamb,/ its fleece was white as snow,/ everywhere that Mary went,/ The lamb was sure to ___," and so on. Gradually use more difficult poetry as your child masters this.

24. **Make a pinwheel.** First, cut a four-inch square of paper, and let your child color both sides with different colors or designs. Now cut diagonally toward the center, beginning at each corner. With each cut, *stop* a half-inch from the center, so that your sheet of paper remains in one piece. Now bend alternating corners toward the middle, fastening them with a straight pin.

When all four corners are fastened, stick the pin through a plastic straw or the eraser of a pencil. For safety, bend the pin as it comes through the back of the eraser and cover the sharp point with heavy tape. Now wave the pinwheel and watch it whirl.

 25. Make curds and whey. Kids will love sampling this old-fashioned dish made famous by Little Miss Muffet. Warm two cups of milk over medium heat until it bubbles. Stir. Remove it from the heat and stir in one tablespoon of vinegar. This will make the milk curdle. Pour the mixture through a strainer into a pot. The whey will flow into the pot and the curds (similar to cottage cheese) will stay in the strainer. Salt it if you wish, and taste some. If you like, you can even act out Little Miss Muffet.

26. Learn about energy. Find things in your house that need energy to work. Older kids can tell you what *kind* of energy: gas, electric, solar? Check out the refrigerator, TV, light bulb, and plants.

27. Make water run uphill. Here's how to do this amazing feat: Stand two glasses side by side, and fill one with water. Now drape a strip of towel from one glass into the other. This strip will act as a wick, and overnight the water will travel from one glass to another, going uphill during part of its journey.

28. **Grow sprouts.** This discovery works very quickly, but you will need to observe its progress for a few days.

Use a clean, empty jar with a wide mouth. Fill it with *damp* paper towels or a damp sponge. Be careful not to pack the jar too tightly. The towels should just press *lightly* against the sides of the glass. Now insert some seeds between the glass and the towels. (Good seeds to try are: a variety of beans, citrus fruits, corn, peas, squash, pear, and apple.) Keep the towels moist by drizzling water onto them each day. Within a day or two, you'll notice sprouts and roots.

When leafy stems have pushed up into the air, tip the jar on its side. Within a day you'll notice that the stems have bent so that the sprout is still reaching straight up. The roots have also curved in order to grow straight down. Explain to older kids that a growth hormone within the plant controls this, and the process is called geotropism.

29. **Test your sense of touch.** Gather identical pairs of several items to put into a paper sack. Some suggestions are: two quarters, two buttons, two toothbrushes, two cotton balls, and two bolts. Have your child reach into a bag and pull out two identical objects.

This tests—and sharpens—kids' sense of touch.

30. **Make paper airplanes.**
Here's a basic folding pattern to try: fold a sheet of typing paper lengthwise down the center. Now fold each top corner, so that they meet in the center. (Your page should look like a house with a pointed roof.) Now fold the *sides* of the paper so that they meet in the center. Crease the new folds. Bring the sides in toward the center one more time and again crease the folds. When you first folded the page in half, you made a crease

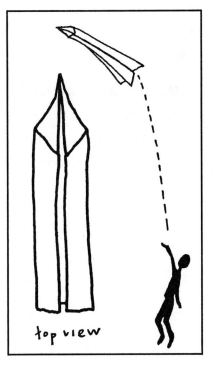

top view

that naturally folds inward as you look at the page. Now fold it the opposite way, so that all the folds you've just created form the wings of your flier. Hold the bottom flaps against the body and sail that baby through the air!

Try attaching a paper clip to the nose of your plane, and see if this added weight changes the way your plane flies. (And for the sake of teachers everywhere, remind kids that airplanes are not for the classroom!)

31. **Make flying saucers.** Graduate from making airplanes to creating flying saucers. Color the back of a paper plate, and sail it like a Frisbee. Advanced artists can draw space aliens peering out of the saucer's tiny windows. (Plastic and cardboard lids work well, too.)

1. **Create a blossoming tree.** Celebrate spring by making your own blooming tree. Draw a tree trunk with lots of extending branches. Now glue your blossoms—popped corn—to the branches.

2. **Weave spring baskets.** Kids can quickly create original designs using the green plastic containers that strawberries and cherry tomatoes are sold in. Give them short strips of brightly colored tissue paper or construction paper. They're easy to thread in and out of the basket's spaces. Older kids can use real hemp from a craft store, to create more traditional baskets. Fill them with grass and treats for lovely gifts.

3. **Make colors.** Cut a red cabbage in half, then slice it into smaller chunks. Boil the cabbage in about a pint of water (the amounts are not critical), and pour the purplish-blue water into several clear, heat-resistant glasses or measuring cups.

Now the magic begins. Add a spoonful of baking soda to one glass and watch what happens to the color. Add a spoonful of vinegar to another glass. What color does *that* make? What color do you get when you pour the two together? (With this experiment you should get brilliant blues and greens with baking soda, and deep reds and bright pinks with vinegar.)

4. **Count your teeth.** Talk about the differences between primary and secondary teeth. Explain that larger molars in the back are what we use for chewing while the incisors in the front do the biting. Talk about what happens when the primary or "baby" teeth fall out and adult, permanent teeth come in. How many rules of good dental hygiene can your child name?

5. **Paint with water.** Create some pictures on the sidewalk using a brush dipped in water. If it's a hot day, you'll need to work fast, or your masterpieces will disappear before they're finished! Explain evaporation—how the sun heats the water and turns it into vapor, which in turn rises and forms clouds.

6. **Make summer butterflies.** Remember the winter butterflies you made in discovery number four in February? Now you can make some summer butterflies by dripping globs of finger paint, or

any other thick paint, onto a folded sheet of construction paper. We like to use the finger paints that come in squeezable tubes for this, plus a dash of glitter. Press firmly to crease the paper and smear the paint onto both sides. When you open it, you'll see a butterfly that's pretty enough to frame!

 7. **Design a family flag.** This project is great because it emphasizes the closeness and stability of the family.

First, let your child help to design and sketch a family flag on a sheet of paper. This can be whatever she likes, or whatever best represents your family unit. Try using each family member's favorite color somewhere on the flag, or if your family loves sports, include silhouettes of tennis racquets or whatever you like to play. Musical notes, interesting geometric shapes, hearts, rainbows, ribbons, stars, animals, vines, and initials are all ways to express your own special personality or history.

You can create your family flag on fabric, and sew it into a pillow or quilt, or fly it like a banner. The family flag can become place mats, a wall hanging, or a holiday ornament. Non-sewing families can use felt and piece their flag together with glue. Try decorating holiday cards, stationery, or T-shirts with your flag.

 8. **Make gelatin oranges.** Cut an orange in half, and remove the pulp, leaving just the rind. Now fill each half with orange gelatin, and chill. This afternoon, after the gelatin has set, slice each half again, to make quarters. Now you can enjoy "orange sections" with your kids. These are fun party foods, and you can make them with lemons and limes, too!

9. **Do pantomimes.** Let one person mime an action while everyone else guesses what he's doing. Here are some suggestions for your mimes: getting into a car and driving, wrapping a gift, painting a wall, getting dressed, reading a book, cutting a sheet of paper, drinking a glass of water, and licking an ice-cream cone.

10. **Make a balloon "sing."** Inflate a balloon, but instead of tying a knot in it, stretch the neck. The balloon will "sing" as air escapes.

 11. **Make soda floats.** Use vanilla ice cream, plus any flavor of soda your child likes. Kids seem to like root beer, orange, and lemon-lime best.

The way to make a float least foamy is to drop in the ice cream *after* you've poured the soda. But do it both ways so your kids can see the difference (and laugh in delight when the foam overflows!).

12. **Practice listening.** Are you a good listener? Pay attention to sounds inside and around your home. Ask your child to name everything she hears. Older kids can make a list of what they hear, while you do the same. Set a timer and in two minutes see if the children were even better listeners than Mom or Dad. Did they hear things you missed?

13. **Make silly moustaches.** Cut a moustache shape from cardboard or stiff paper. (Be sure to leave two small tabs and a dip on top, so that you can attach the moustache to your nostrils!) Pretend to be characters such as Groucho Marx, Charlie Chaplin, or a dastardly villain.

14. **Build a marshmallow kingdom.** Using toothpicks and large or tiny marshmallows, construct buildings and objects. Your creations will resemble Tinker Toy constructions! If you don't want to use marshmallows, garbanzo beans work just as well.

 Begin a seven-day series on Polynesia. This region includes Hawaii, Tahiti, Samoa, Fiji, New Zealand, and many other islands.

15. **Make leis.** Explain that most leis are made from fragrant flowers, but some are made from shells, seeds, feathers, and nuts. On many islands when someone puts a lei around your neck, they also give you a kiss!

Using a *long* strip of crepe paper, and a needle and thread, you can make beautiful leis. To start, thread the needle with enough thread to form a long necklace. Sew stitches about an inch apart, right down the center of the crepe paper strip. As you sew, gather and fold the crepe paper onto the thread in accordion fashion; it will start to twist and form a column of color. Stack your crepe paper folds fairly tightly, and before long you'll have a great-looking lei!

16. **Build a beach.** Polynesian islands are known for their dazzling beaches. Your child can create a picture of a beach by using blue paint for the water, then gluing sand and shells onto the land part. (You don't even need real shells; cut tiny copies from construction paper or use macaroni shells.) Talk about how shells are actually the homes of sea animals. Have your child draw a starfish on the beach, and explain that they aren't really fish at all, but echinoderms, and have no brain. Did you know that if you cut a starfish in two, each half may regenerate into a new starfish?

17. **Make a cucumber catamaran.** Explain to your kids that these swiftly moving boats were once the Polynesians' only means of inter-island travel. They were made from wood and also used for fishing.

You can make your own vessel with a zucchini or cucumber. Parboil the cucumber so it's easier to scoop out the seeds. Slice it in half lengthwise, and use a spoon to scoop out the seeds and most of the flesh (use them later if you wish). Make a stiff paper sail and attach it to the canoes with toothpicks. Arrange the two cucumber slices side by side, and hold them parallel with toothpicks. Now test your boat to see if it will sail.

18. **Make a fruit salad.** Since this series is about the islands, try to use only the fruits that grow there. Include chunks of pineapple, coconut, papaya, kiwi, mango, guava, and orange. Serve the salad in a coconut or pineapple half, if you wish.

19. **Bang a drum.** Explain that Tahitian dancing is known for the prominence of drumbeats. Authentic island drums are made of wood, shells, animal skins, and other natural materials. Consult your child about

what household materials you can use to make your own set of drums. Shoeboxes and empty oatmeal boxes work pretty well.

20. **Weave place mats.** Polynesian weaving is found in floor

coverings, clothing, baskets, bedding, walls, and artwork. Demonstrate weaving to kids with long strips of colored paper or long, narrow plant leaves. Place several strips parallel on a table, and help your child weave over, under, over, under with another strip. Pick up the next strip, and weave the opposite way: under, over, under, over. Keep going until you've woven a rectangle.

21. **Make a volcano** and finish the Polynesia series with a bang. Explain that the island were formed by volcanoes, and that many volcanoes around the world are still active. Here's how to make one: Sculpt a cone-shape from clay, about a foot high. You can also make a cone from newspapers to form the body of the volcano. (Stuff this cone with crumpled paper to keep it from collapsing.) Fasten this "mountain" to a cardboard base. Be sure to leave a little indentation in the top, as this is where your lava will

erupt from. Now rest half an empty eggshell in the indentation, and fill it with two teaspoons of baking soda. Make the lava by drizzling vinegar onto the soda. It should foam, bubble, and erupt. This is great fun!

This concludes the Polynesia series.

22. **Decorate flowerpots.** Glue rope or colored yarn to the exterior of an inexpensive clay flowerpot, a can, or any other suitable container. Wrap the rope in tight rows around the container, or swirl it into a design. Later, when the glue has dried, you can paint the pot or leave it natural. Clear nail polish or shellac can give it a bright shine. These make great gifts for grandparents.

23. **Make a hand puppet.** Make a loose fist with your thumb tucked in. The space on the side of your fist, between your thumb and finger, becomes the mouth. Draw lips here. Draw eyes on the knuckle of your index finger. Kids love these, and enjoy talking in a funny voice for their puppets.

24. **Bend light.** As you immerse a straw or pencil in a glass of water, ask your child to tell you what's happening to the straw. Is it broken? Is it bending? Explain that water can bend light, making a stick appear crooked.

25. **Make a sound.** Use ordinary objects around the house to make interesting sound effects. Some ideas: scrunch cornstarch in your hand to simulate footsteps in the snow; shake paper clips in an empty metal bandage box to simulate a train; wrinkle cellophane for the sound of fire; splash water in a bowl to sound like swimming. Experiment with other sounds, and perhaps put on your own radio drama.

26. **Draw flags of your nationality.** Look up the flags of the countries of your heritage, using a book from the library or an encyclopedia. Let your child draw and color them.

27. **Make a pirate's treasure map.** Hide a treasure for your child ahead of time. Draw a treasure map with directions, arrows, landmarks, and an X to mark the spot, of course.

Roll up the map so it looks like a scroll, or brush tea over it to give it an antique look. Now see if your child can follow the map to each landmark until he reaches the hiding place.

28. **Uncork a bottle without touching the cork.** Begin with an empty, clean bottle and a cork that fits snugly. Uncork the bottle

and pour in a tablespoon of baking soda. Now add one-third cup of vinegar and *quickly* cork the bottle. Watch as the soda and vinegar create gas. The pressure of the gas will force the cork up.

29. **Make a balloon-propulsion boat.**
Here's how: First cut the back off a clean, empty milk carton. Now cut a two-inch slit in the bottom of the carton, beginning at the edge that's been cut and heading toward the center. Blow up a balloon and put its neck in the slit so that it's *almost* pinched closed. Let the rest of the balloon sit inside the empty milk carton. As air escapes from the balloon, it will blow out the back of your "boat," propelling the milk carton across a bathtub or sink filled with water.

30. **Compose yourself.** Today you'll make up your own songs. Kids love to invent both the melody and the lyrics. Older kids can make up songs about specific things—the family, their pets, a favorite toy or activity. Think of a jazzy song, a sad song, a funny song, even a rap song!

31. **Make a cookbook.** Have your kids draw pictures of what they like to eat, and describe the "recipe" to you. Write it down below their illustration. The results are quite hilarious, and a collection of recipes makes a wonderful cookbook. Grandparents will demand copies!

1. **Don't pop the balloon!** Can you stick a needle into a balloon without breaking the balloon? Blow up three or four, and let your child experiment with various ways of doing this. Then, on the last balloon, show her how it's done: You simply pierce the balloon where it is least stretched—right near the knot. An even trickier way of piercing the balloon is to put a piece of transparent tape on the surface. If you stick the needle through the tape, the balloon won't pop.

2. **Go bowling.** Ahead of time, save six to ten empty plastic soda bottles or milk cartons. (You can also use empty tissue boxes or cardboard tubes.) Arrange the bottles like bowling pins, with one in front, two behind, three behind that, and so on. Use any ball to knock them over. Save the "pins" to bowl again another time.

3. **Curl dandelion stems.** For those who think weeds have no redeeming features, here's a project that uses dandelions. First,

you'll need to gather some. They're usually everywhere during warm months, but if there are none nearby, you might need to take a nature walk the day before. Be sure the dandelions have stems that are at least three inches long. Slit the stems into several strips by pulling them from the bottom end toward the blossom. (The strips should remain attached to the blossom.) Now immerse the flowers in cold water and watch the stems curl up.

4. **Ride a magic carpet.** Spread out a towel or blanket and sit cross-legged on it. As you imagine the carpet rising into the sky, look below. What do you see? Does everything look tiny? Where is the carpet taking you?

5. **Be an inventor.** Have your kids invent a gadget or machine for the future. Draw pictures of the invention. This gets kids acquainted with problem-solving and gives their imaginations free rein.

One of my sons invented an airplane that uses smog for fuel so it can clean the air as it flies along. Not a bad idea!

6. **Give back rubs and massages.** Let your child feel on your back how muscle is different from bone. Talk about the spine and ribs. If possible, show him an encyclopedia or library book picture of the anatomy of the back, and where the muscles lie. Let your

child experience how relaxing a massage can be.

7. **Blow bubbles.** A solution of dishwashing liquid and water makes the best bubble potion ever. Use a pie tin and a bent hanger (or a plastic cup and a bubble stick from a commercial bottle) to blow your bubbles.

Do this outside, of course, and see who can blow the biggest bubble, the smallest bubble, the highest floating bubble, and the longest-before-it-pops bubble.

8. **Make a crepe-paper collage.** Tear up various colors of crepe paper and glue the pieces onto a sheet of paper. Sprinkle some water onto your creation, and watch the colors run. You now have both a collage and a watercolor creation.

9. **Hang a spoon from your nose.** This one guarantees some giggles. Simply place the concave side against your nose.

10. **Play musical straws.** Flatten one end of a plastic straw, so that about one inch will stay flat. Using safety scissors, cut the flat end into a v-shaped point. This simulates the reed used in many musical instruments. Put the pointed end in your mouth (but don't

press too hard), and blow. Experiment with different lengths of straw; the shorter pieces will be higher pitched.

11. **Learn about bees.** Encourage your child to buzz and "fly" around the room. You may want to play a recording of "The Flight of the Bumblebee" by Rimsky-Korsakov (available from your library).

Taste some honey. Explain that bees help to pollinate flowers by transferring pollen, which sticks to their hairy bodies, to the pistil of a flower.

Make a bee, using black and yellow pipe cleaners. Wrap a spiral of alternating colors around a finger, then slip it off. Glue on paper wings.

12. **Keep your balance.** Have your child stand with his heels against the wall. Place an object at his feet. Can he pick it up without moving his feet? Not without falling over!

13. **Learn about measurements.** Play in a sink filled with water, using containers of various sizes. Learn about cups, pints, quarts, gallons, tablespoons and teaspoons. Guess how many teaspoons in a tablespoon, then measure and find out. Even older kids will be surprised.

14. **Let's trade coats.** Place ten pennies in a bowl. Stir in one-quarter cup vinegar and one teaspoon salt. Drop in a clean iron nail. Overnight, the nail will have a shiny copper coating! This vinegar and salt solution dissolves some of the copper molecules, which attach themselves to the iron nail.

15. **Wash your bike or the car.** Give it a quick spray and rubdown. Make it sparkle! If washing a car or bike is impractical for you, how about washing some other toy that has long gone unbathed? Teach kids that it's important to take care of their property and clean the things that get dirty.

 Begin a seven-day series on the American Frontier. Explain that the frontier shaped American culture and brought opportunity and adventure to the pioneers. Because settlers were isolated, they became more creative and self-reliant.

16. **Learn to tie knots.** With help from a library book, show kids various knots used by cowboys on the range. Or let kids make up knots of their own and give them creative names. Older kids can try to spin a lasso.

17. **Make pottery.** Many Native Americans fashioned all their

cookware from clay, which was easy to come by. Much Native American pottery is decorative and artistic.

Make the clay for your pottery the night before. Mix one cup of cornstarch, two cups of baking soda, and one-quarter cup of cold water in a saucepan. Add a few drops of coloring if you wish. Stir over medium heat until the mixture thickens to a paste. This takes just a few minutes. Keep the clay covered with a damp cloth until cool. Store it in a sealed bag in the fridge; when you're ready to use it, knead it into a pliable consistency. Now press and pinch the clay into little pots or sculptures. When your pottery is dry, you can paint or shellac it.

18. **Make moccasins.** You can use chamois leather, towels, vinyl, heavy fabric, whatever's on hand, to create these shoes worn by Native Americans. The pattern is easy to make: Trace your child's foot on the fabric, leaving an extra inch all around. Now trace just the upper half of that same foot, and this piece will become the top of the shoe. Cut a long strip of fabric that's one or two inches wide, and this will become the side of the shoe. Sew it together with yarn or leather shoelaces. Repeat the process for the other

foot, and you'll have quickly crafted a pair of moccasins. (An alternative to sewing is using a glue gun, an appliance you'll wonder how you lived without after you own one.) You can make these moccasins in advance to decorate later. Kids can decorate their shoes with drawings, or even sew on tiny beaded designs. For a real quick fix, make mock moccasins by decorating a pair of white socks.

19. **Make a raft.** Glue together popsicle sticks, or any other kinds of sticks, to make a small raft. See if it will float.

Explain how people living on the frontier tied logs together to make rafts for transportation. Then older kids can carve canoes from soft wood.

20. **Create sand paintings.** Many Native American tribes make beautiful sand paintings. To create one, collect various colors of dry dirt and sand. (You may want to start doing this ahead of time, while you're visiting places away from home.) You can make your own colored "sand" by rubbing colored chalk against coarse sandpaper. Now, using a clear jar, alternate pouring layers of sand and dirt into the jar to make an interesting pattern. You can actually get your painting to look like mountains, a sunset, or just a geometric pattern.

21. **Make a guitar.** Stretch rubber bands over an open, shallow box. Pretend to sit around the campfire and sing some songs, just like real ranch hands. Talk about life at the ranch and all the hard work that's done there: driving cattle over long distances, branding them, tending sick cattle, roping, navigating rough terrain, and repairing fences. A lot of time is also spent training dogs. Many ranchers pay hundreds of dollars for good cattle dogs who can herd cows out of thick brush.

22. **Have a barbecue.** Pretend you've just had a hard day of herding cattle. Heat up some miniature hot dogs in barbecue sauce. Try some cornbread or canned stew. Smaller kids can pretend to gallop in and tie their horses to a hitching post before sitting down to some hearty "grub."

This concludes the American Frontier series.

23. **Learn about antibodies.** We all have antibodies to help us fight germs. Vaccinations help our bodies form antibodies so we don't get certain diseases. To show kids how antibodies work, cut the center from a slice of bread, using a cookie cutter. The center now represents the germ, and the outside part is the antibody You can see how the outside part can perfectly trap the germ

Antibodies fight in many ways to render germs harmless. When you are injected with the measles vaccine, for example, you make antibodies in just the right shape to fight measles germs, should they invade.

If you want, slice two pieces of bread at once, and make sandwiches out of the new shapes for the kids to take to school.

24. **Paint a face.** Using watercolors, try some face-painting today. Does your child want to be a cat, a clown, a rainbow princess, or a scary monster? (Wash off the paint before she heads for school.)

25. **Study spider webs.** Who can find the most spider webs outside? Watch how a spider builds one, if you can. Explain how spider webs work, and that spiders help us by eating bugs that are harmful to gardens.

26. **Balance a salt shaker.** Balance a salt shaker in just a few granules of salt. Begin with a salt shaker (or a drinking glass) that is squared at the bottom, instead of rounded. Place the shaker on an angle in a small pile of salt on a flat surface. When the shaker is

standing on its own, blow away the excess crystals. You'll see that just a few crystals are holding the entire shaker in place.

27. **Make bells.** Tie two spoons to the middle of a long piece of string. Hold one end of the string in each hand and put the ends up to your ears. Swing the string so that the spoons strike each other. The sound traveling up the string will sound like chimes.

28. **Find a worm.** Look for worms outside. (You may have to stage this ahead of time by buying one at a nursery or bait store and planting it outside.) Discuss how worms help gardens to thrive by loosening the soil.

Return the worm to its favorite spot and watch it burrow in.

29. **Learn about slope and speed.** Explain that the greater the slope, the faster the speed. Roll a toy car or a can down a board, which you've propped up on a stack of books or a low stool. Prop the board up higher, on the seat of a chair. Watch how much faster the car goes now.

30. **Be a sidewalk artist.** Go outside and practice writing letters and numbers. Use colored chalk. Play hopscotch! Notice that the chalk gets used up more quickly on rougher surfaces.

31. **Launch Noah's ark.** Draw Noah's art at the bottom of a sheet of paper. Now glue on animal crackers in matching pairs. Paint them colors, if you like. Older kids can add elaborate scenery, and even write a poem about animals, Noah, or rainbows.

Celebrate American independence with this six-day series.

1. **Draw an American flag.** Even tiny kids love to hear about Betsy Ross and our flag, and then watch for flags waving in the neighborhood. Younger kids can sketch and color one while older kids try to sew one or learn the proper way to fold one. Scout manuals and library books can help.

2. **Listen to patriotic music.** If you have none, sing a few of our country's patriotic songs. Talk about what patriotism means, and , why you feel proud of your country.

3. **Make paper hats.** Create hats out of newspapers or large sheets of blank newsprint. Fold a large sheet of paper in half, width-wise. Holding it so the fold is on top, make a vertical crease down the center, then open this fold. Now bring the top corners down to meet each other at this crease and press the new folds

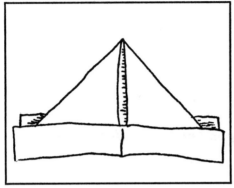

flat. You have just formed the triangular top of the hat. Bring the narrow pieces below, up on each side to form the brim and press again. These are similar to hats worn by American colonists.

Pretend to be Revolutionary War soldiers. Kids can decorate the hats while you tell the story of Paul Revere, or read Longfellow's classic poem, "Paul Revere's Ride." Explain that at midnight, Paul Revere rode through the streets of Lexington on a borrowed horse warning the people, "The British are coming!" Discuss the importance of the Revolution and how colonists fought for independence from Britain.

4. **March in a parade.** Using homemade instruments, or pots and pans, march around the house in a Fourth of July parade.

 5. **Make an ice-cream pie.** Fill a prepared graham cracker crust with softened ice cream. Get creative if you want, and use strawberry, vanilla and blueberry ice cream or frozen yogurt for a red-white-and-blue effect.

A recipe I like blends a half-gallon of softened vanilla ice cream with a small can of undiluted, frozen lemonade concentrate. Spoon it into the pie crust, and freeze.

6. **Play statue.** Twirl each other around, and then "freeze" in whatever position you land in. Guess what each person looks like. If you wish, tell your kids about the Statue of Liberty. Explain that it was a gift from France to celebrate our country's one hundredth year of independence.

This concludes the American independence series.

7. **Share a biblical or historical story.** Tell your child about an inspiring character from the Bible or history. Act it out, if you wish. Emphasize what's important about this person's actions and ask your child to think about it during the day. Tonight, see if he has any comments.

8. **Play bingo with shapes and colors.** Ahead of time make small bingo boards using stiff paper or cardboard. Write B-I-N-G-O across the top, then form five vertical columns by drawing lines between the letters. Draw five horizontal lines. Sketch a star or some other symbol in the center to indicate a free space and in the remaining squares draw or write something the child needs to

learn, such as letters, shapes, or colors.

When you're ready to play, follow the basic rules of bingo: Call out the letter above the column and the name of an object in a square (G–circle or b–triangle). The kids can place a marker over that picture if they have it. (You can use buttons, dry cereal, or pennies for markers.)

Make the game more advanced by putting numbers in the squares. Then call out equations such as, "What's 12 minus 7?" "What's 50 divided by 5?" As soon as your child covers every square in one row, she gets to shout, "Bingo!"

9. **Paint or draw to music.** Don't just turn on the radio; preselect music with distinct moods. Choose songs that are fast and wild, soothing and peaceful, rollicking and fun. See what type of drawing your child creates or what colors he selects with each song. Afterward, talk about how the music made your child feel, and what he was thinking as he drew.

10. **What's that smell?** The night before you do this project, fill

several small jars with spices and other substances with distinct and strong scents. Try lemon juice, vinegar, perfume, cinnamon, vanilla, onion, rubbing alcohol, motor oil, extracts, and spices. Blindfold your child and see if she guesses correctly.

You can also ask your child to think of words that describe the smells. Don't be surprised to hear unusual descriptions such as "prickly," "scary," "bright," or "happy." These represent memories or feelings associated with certain smells.

11. **Looking for letters.** Find all the letters in your name in an old magazine and circle them. Older kids can race the clock to do it faster and faster, beating their previous records.

12. **Here today, here tomorrow?** Gather small bits of food, plastic, paper, cloth, wood, and metal. Now go outside and bury each of these items. Over the next few weeks, some of the items will decompose and others will not, showing kids firsthand what biodegradable means. Which materials does your child think will decompose fastest? Which will not decompose at all?

In a few weeks dig up the items, and check to see what happened. When kids see that plastic is not biodegradable, they may become more conscious of recycling plastic bottles. Older kids might even like to start a compost pile. Using any size bin, alternate layers of dirt and organic material, such as grass clippings or leaves. Over time, the organic material will decompose, mix with the dirt, and provide rich planting soil.

13. **Take a safari.** Pretend you're looking through binoculars at your child as she pretends to be the African animals you name: giraffe, baboon, zebra, crocodile, elephant. Last, find the King of the Jungle, a lion. Now switch roles. Older kids can learn the names of Africa's countries and find them on a map.

14. **Weave a Greek wreath.** Make a wreath for your head using leaves and grasses. An art book showing sculptures which include this wreath can inspire you.

15. **Shell peas.** There's something wonderfully homey and down-on-the-farm about shelling peas. Kids will love popping open the pods and chasing the bouncing peas. You can cook them to serve at dinner tonight, but they're just as tasty and nutritious when eaten raw.

16. **Make postcards.** Paste magazine pictures on a three-by-five-inch card. Then write a message on the back and mail it!

17. **Make a water wheel.** Snip one-inch cuts into a paper plate, all around the edge and about two inches apart. Bend a little flap at each cut. Each flap should be bent in the same direction. Now push a pencil through the center of the plate and hold the plate's edge under a running faucet. The force of the water should spin your plate just like a water wheel.

18. **Make ice-cube necklaces.** Fill an ice-cube tray with water the night before, and drape a string over the cubes. In the morning, when you pop out the frozen ice cubes, they'll all be connected by the string. What a wonderful way to cool off on a hot summer day!

19. **Play hero and villain.** Act out a quick melodrama. Fake moustaches, wigs, and a cape can add to the fun but aren't necessary. Have a villain ("You must pay the rent"); a maiden in distress ("But I cannot pay the rent"); and a hero ("I will pay the rent!"). Each person can play more than one role, if necessary. Don't forget to hiss, boo, and cheer.

20. **Find your way around a circle.** Trace a plate or use a

compass to make a circle on a sheet of paper. Draw a line from the outer edge of the circle to its center. Explain that this line marks the circle's radius. Now continue the line to the other side of the circle to show the diameter. Measure it to illustrate that the diameter is twice the radius.

Find other circular shapes in the house and have your child trace the radius and diameter with his finger. If you wish, draw a giant circle outside with chalk and have your child walk the radius and diameter. You can also slice a pie to show this idea. Older kids can guess where the center of a circle is and then measure it precisely to see if their guess was on target.

 21. **Make cool clowns.** Place a scoop of ice cream on a saucer, then top it with an upside-down sugar cone for a hat. Press colorful candies onto the ice cream for facial features, or pipe frosting onto the hat for ruffles and polka dots. Freeze for a fun after-school snack. These make great party treats, too.

 22. **Have a boat race.** You can make boats from cardboard, wood, empty thread spools—anything that floats will do. Cut a tiny paper sail and attach it to your boat with a toothpick. Now in a shallow bathtub, place your boats at one end, and shout "Go!"

You can blow on the sails, if you want, and let your child make the rules for this race. Older kids can make very elaborate boats, while younger ones might like to keep it simple and decorate their creations with crayons.

23. **Be anteaters.** Or at least popcorn eaters. Place a piece of popcorn on your shoulder, then turn your head and stick out your tongue until it touches the kernel. Can you "catch" the popcorn on the tip of your tongue? Laughter is inevitable, but if you laugh too hard, you'll blow the popcorn away!

 Begin a six-day series on outer space and explore the Earth and its neighbors.

24. **How big is the Earth?** Ask your child to guess how big the Earth would be if the sun were the size of a basketball. (Earth would be about the size of a pea since the sun is more than a hundred times bigger than the Earth.)

Some other ideas: Draw a diagram of the solar system, or look at an artist's rendering in a book. Learn the names of the planets. Pretend that you are the sun while your kids orbit around you. Now switch roles and let them be the sun. Ask questions such as, "Which planet is your favorite?" or "Which planet would you most like to visit?"

25. **Learn about stars' colors.** Our sun is a star and stars are great masses of burning gas. Draw and color stars, arranging them from coolest to hottest. (The coolest stars are red, then orange, yellow, yellow-white, white, and then blue-white.) Our sun is yellow. What would happen to us if our sun were blue-white? Red?

26. **Discover the moon.** The moon has always been a popular theme in poetry, literature, and music. Talk about some of the reasons for that. You can discuss its familiar "face" and tell your child that people used to think it was made of cheese. Explain the phases of the moon and the belief that mysterious things are said to happen when it's full.

Can your child think of any songs or books that mention the moon? How about writing a poem or song of your own?

27. **Take a moon walk.** Tell kids that the first person to walk on the moon was Neil Armstrong in 1969. Walk like you're in a bulky astronaut suit. Move in slow motion and explain that you weigh less on the moon because of a weaker gravitational pull. (This means you can jump a lot higher!)

Try creating a spacesuit by cutting a face window in a paper bag and wearing it over your head. Older kids can talk about the latest space mission and the prospect of people living in space someday. Would your kids volunteer to go up into space? Why or why not?

28. **Eat space food.** Inexpensive dehydrated ice cream and french fries are available in foil pouches in museum gift shops, camping supply stores, and educational/discovery toy stores. Mix with hot water and enjoy! You can also find orange drink mixes and food in tubes, such as peanut butter. Talk about the lifestyle you'd have aboard a spaceship, how you'd sleep, exercise, communicate with Earth, wash, relax, and work.

29. **Create a new planet.** Draw a diagram of the solar system and have your child draw a new planet. What is this new planet's name? Can it sustain life? What is it like there?

This concludes the outer space series.

30. **Make a long-distance phone call.** Phone a relative as a surprise. Alexander Graham Bell, a teacher of the deaf, invented the telephone in 1876. His assistant, Thomas A. Watson, heard the first telephone transmission when Bell spilled some battery acid on his clothes and said, "Mr. Watson, come here. I want you!" Watson

heard the transmission in another room.

31. **Go fishing with paper and magnets.** (You won't even have to bait your hook!) Here's how: Cut out several paper fish and let your child color them if he wishes. Put paper clips on the fish, over their mouths. Now spread the fish out on the floor. Tie a string to a pencil and attach a magnet to the end. Dangle the magnet over the paper clips and see what kinds of fish you can catch!

A variation is to cut your fish from a folded sheet of paper, so that kids can open them up and find a surprise inside. You can write numbers (Who can fish for the highest score?), riddles, fortunes, household chores to do, loving messages, silly requests ("Do a somersault"), or the names of charades to act out.

1. **How hot?** Help your child draw a thermometer with lines and numbers. She can guess what today's temperature will be and use red to mark it on the thermometer. Take your own temperatures, if you like. (Let's hope you don't discover that somebody has a fever!)

 2. **Dry flowers.** You can use the microwave oven to do this, or just let the flowers sit in silicon for several days.

Here's the fastest way: It's best to work with one flower at a time Place the flower you'd like to dry in a cardboard box. Very gently, pour silicon crystals (available in most craft stores) in and around the blossoms you want to preserve. Microwave for thirty seconds at a time. Carefully blow away the crystals to check the results.

Some flowers, such as baby's breath and statice, dry naturally in the air. A florist can give you some tips on which varieties to choose. Older children can arrange their dried flowers under a glass dome, gluing the stems to a wooden base beneath the dome. These make lovely gifts or decorations

3. **Make lemonade.** Very few people make lemonade from scratch anymore, but it's really simple. Squeeze the juice from one or two lemons into a pitcher. Dilute with water, and add sugar and ice cubes. As a variation, try limeade or add food coloring. These are perfect summertime thirst-quenchers.

4. **Guess what's been moved.** Close your eyes while your child moves something in the room. Now open your eyes and guess what's been relocated. Switch roles.

5. **See the world.** Study a globe or a map of the world. Point out the seven continents. Some scientists believe the continents used to fit together like puzzle pieces. Can you find any land masses that look as though they might fit together? How many countries can you find and name?

6. **Explore taste and smell.** Show kids how our sense of taste is closely connected to our sense of smell. Slice an apple and a potato. Now blindfold your child and have him pinch his nose closed. Ask him to taste each food and see if he can tell them apart without smelling them.

7. **Be a jumping bean.** Jump from one spot to another, then measure the distance. Try to beat your own records. You can do this outside or indoors.

8. **Let it rain.** Create a mini rain shower in your kitchen. Place a few ice cubes in a frying pan, then hold it above a pot of boiling water. As the steam rises, it will condense against the bottom of the cold frying pan, forming drops that will rain back into the pot.

9. **Follow me.** How are your kids at following directions? Give them some crayons and paper, then say, "Draw a red circle with a yellow box inside." Or, "Draw a red house with two windows, a door, and two trees. Do it in that order." Make the directions more and more complicated for older kids. Some children can't remember more than one or two directions at a time, and they confuse which to do first. This is good practice.

10. **Make cream-pops.** Prepare pudding ahead of time (instant pudding makes this easy). Let your kids pour it into popsicle forms or regular cups. (If you use cups, insert popsicle sticks.) Now put them in the freezer, and this afternoon you can all enjoy a frosty, rich treat!

11. **Create balloon messages.** In advance, write secret messages on small scraps of paper. Now fold up the papers and insert them into balloons. Blow up the balloons and tie them. Let your child pop the balloons and then do whatever the paper says: "Hug your mom," "sing a song," or "tell a joke." This is a fun party game, too.

12. **Fatten up some raisins.** Let your child drop a few raisins into a bowl of hot water. Keep it in a warm place, and check on it over the next few days. Water will pass through the skin and the raisins will plump up.

 Begin an eight-day series on Europe. Show your child the countries of Europe on a map.

13. **Take a whirlwind tour of Europe's tastes and smells.** On a countertop, line up some favorite European delights for your child to visit. He can smell French perfume, sample Swiss chocolate, smell Italian spices, sniff an English tea rose, and taste some European cheeses.

14. **Make windmills.** Describe the beautiful windmills of Holland and then create one. First,

cut the windmill's blades from a stiff piece of paper. Now punch a hole near the top of one side of an empty, clean milk carton. Fasten the blades to your carton with a brass brad, poking it through the hole that you made. Make sure the blades will spin, and you've got a Dutch windmill! Windmills harness wind power and were used in the Netherlands to drain water from the soaked ground. Today most are used to pump water and to generate electricity.

15. **Be a matador.** Tell kids about the bullfights that take place in Spain. One person can swing the cape (a towel), while the other holds her fingers like the horns of a bull and charges through the towel. Be sure the matador shouts *"Toro, Toro!"* while the "crowd" roars *"Olé!"*

16. **Make castles.** Use wet sand or clay to sculpt a castle. Talk about what it must have been like to live in a real castle (Cold and dark!). Show pictures of castles, if you have any. Why did they need to be fortified? Do they all have a drawbridge? What is a moat? Ask kids if they believe in dragons.

17. **Listen to Europe.** Try to yodel like the

Swiss. Imitate a cuckoo clock; imitate Scottish bagpipes. Play an opera or a symphony that was composed and recorded in Europe. Explain that in some countries, even small towns have opera houses because music is so deeply cherished.

18. **Make a Viking ship.** Tell kids about these Scandinavian sailors and create one of their vessels. You may need to follow a sketch from a library book or encyclopedia. Cut out the silhouette from two pieces of paper. Glue the bottom edges together; you might even cut out small paper Vikings to go inside.

19. **Try some of the dances native to Europe.** Folk dances and polkas are fun. Try the French cancan or the Austrian waltz.

20. **Meet Hans Christian Andersen.** Tell your kids about this famous Danish writer. Ask your child if he thinks he can make up a fairy tale of his own.

This concludes the Europe series.

21. **Draw balloon faces.** Before blowing up a balloon, draw a face on it, using thick, dark markers. The picture will look lighter when the balloon is inflated. Now blow the balloon up slightly and tie it. Squeeze it in different ways to make a big nose or a tiny hat.

22. **Stage an Olympics.** Go outside and let the games begin! Give awards for cartwheels, forward rolls, and jumps. Have your children step onto a stool or sturdy box to receive their prizes. You can present paper certificates or medals cut from construction paper and strung with yarn. Be sure to hum or play the national anthem as your child steps forward to receive the medal.

23. **Cut an eternal loop.** This is called the Möbius strip, named for Ferdinand Möbius, the mathematician who discovered it. It never ceases to amaze young and old.

Here's how you make one: Cut a long strip of paper, at least an inch wide. Next, bend the ends around to form a perfect circle. Just before you tape the two ends together, turn one end over, so your circle looks twisted. Now tape the two ends together. With a pair of safety scissors, cut (or let your child cut) lengthwise down the strip. When you get back to your starting place, you'll see that you have not cut the circle in two, but rather it becomes twice as large. If you cut it down the center again, you'll get two linked Möbius strips, each twice as large as the one you started with.

24. **Learn how to set the table.** Where does the fork go, the spoon, the knife? Older kids can create interesting centerpieces or new ways to fold napkins.

25. **Put pillows in the freezer.** This may very well become a habit during August! Tonight, when it's time for bed, put some pillows in the freezer for a few minutes. Then take them out and let kids savor the chilly results. The pillows don't stay cold for long, but while it lasts . . . ahhhhh. . . .

26. **Play "Penny on a Cloud."** This is a fun game that your kids will request again and again. It's also a great party game.

Place a penny in a measuring cup, then fill the cup with flour. Pack it firmly, then invert it onto a plate. Lift the cup carefully, and the flour should keep its shape, with the penny resting on top. Now, using a dull knife, slice off sections from the sides of the column of flour. Take turns, being careful not to slice too close to the center. Whoever makes the penny fall, loses.

27. **Play "Button Billiards."** Tape eight paper cups to the sides of a table, so that they hang down like pockets on a pool table. Using a pile of 16 buttons, see who can slide them, with a flick of the finger, across the table and into a cup. Let your children make the rules—you can give each person buttons of a different color, or take turns with all the buttons and keep score. You can use one button as a cue ball, or just flick each button directly into the cup.

Look around the house for button substitutes. Some good sliders are coins, dried beans, and checkers.

28. **Learn the states.** Trace or sketch a map of the United States, but don't fill in the names of the States. Let your child point to the region where you live, and if she's old enough, fill in as many state names as she can. (Even most adults can't do this perfectly.)

29. **Create a window-hanging.** Cut two sheets of waxed paper into the same shape (I like to use a big heart) and place crayon crumbs between them. Iron the paper. The crayon crumbs will melt and spread into bright splashes of color. Don't separate the waxed paper. Instead, punch a hole at the top, and hang it from a thread. You've made a beautiful sun-catcher.

30. **Spice up your day.** Put a drop or two of hot pepper sauce on the inside of your wrist. Soon it will almost seem as if your skin can "taste" the hot and spicy flavor of the sauce. Be sure to wash it off when you're through.

31. **Be safe.** You can make this fun by playing "What If?" Draw questions from a hat. Ask kids: What would you do if the house were on fire? What if we were shopping and suddenly you realized

you were all alone? What if Mommy got injured and you couldn't wake her up? What if a stranger came to pick you up from school? Discuss the answers, of course. Help your child understand *why* certain actions are the safest ones.

1. **Make leaf rubbings.** Create your own autumn leaves—before the ones on the trees turn colors. Find several green leaves and cover each one with a sheet of paper. Rub the side of a crayon over the paper. The leaf and its veins will begin to appear on your paper. Do your rubbings in reds, oranges, purples, and other autumn colors. Cut out the leaves and decorate your windows with them. Older kids can also learn to name the parts of the leaf.

2. **Make a telephone.** Punch a hole through the bottoms of two clean, empty cans. Thread a string through each hole, and knot it on the inside, so it won't slip out. Wax the string by rubbing an old candle against it. Now stretch out your phone's cord and speak "long distance." It works best if you keep the string pulled taut.

3. **What's it like outside?** Build your kids' vocabulary outdoors. Head outside and ask your kids to find something around them

that's smooth, rough, hard, soft, or wet. Give older kids more sophisticated adjectives: sinewy, opaque, pungent, spherical, muted, sparse or temporary.

 Begin a five-day series on the Middle East. This area includes Israel, Egypt, Saudi Arabia, Turkey, Pakistan and several other countries.

4. **Wear a turban.** Explain that these are headdresses worn in India and the Middle East to protect men from the sun. They can also indicate social rank. Girls can create saris or veils. Most Indian women wear saris, some made of silk.

5. **Be a snake charmer.** Take turns being the cobra and the snake charmer. Have the snake climb into a large basket, box, or clean garbage can. As the charmer begins playing the flute, the snake can slowly serpentine its way out.

Did you know that snakes are deaf and don't actually hear the music? These creatures are just mimicking the swaying of the snake charmer.

6. **Become mummies.** Using an old sheet, wrap *yourselves* as

mummies. Explain that people, especially in Egypt, used to preserve their dead with special chemicals. These "mummies" were often buried with precious artifacts and scrolls of writing. It was believed the dead would take these treasures with them into the next life.

7. **Build a pyramid.** Use blocks or clay to replicate the amazing Egyptian pyramids. Older kids can study Egyptian art and architecture, and the treasures of the pharaoh Tutankhamen.

8. **Discover the Dead Sea.** Tell kids about the Dead Sea, the salt lake located on the Israel–Jordan border. Explain that its extremely high salt content resulted from the rapid evaporation in the area's hot climate.

Now see how many items that sink in regular water will float in salt water. Start with a raw egg.

You can also tell kids that there used to be a very salty body of water in the United States, too—the Great Salt Lake, in Utah. However, melting snow and flooding have added so much fresh water to the lake, its salt content is only about as much as the ocean. Today, tourists can't float there as they once did.

This concludes the Middle East series.

9. **It's a bug! It's a Martian! It's your kid!** Use pipe cleaners to make colorful antennae. Twist two or three strands together to make a headband, then fasten two more to the sides so that they stick up. Curl the tips.

What else can you make from pipe cleaners? Try jewelry, eyeglasses, animals.

10. **Calling all conductors!** Pull off your socks and stand with one foot on a rug and the other on a bare floor (tile, if possible). Which surface feels coldest? Even though both are the same temperature, the bare floor is a better conductor. It conducts heat away from your skin, and so feels colder than the carpet. Try this experiment with other objects in the room.

11. **Test your reflexes.** Sit down, cross your legs, and have your partner tap just below your kneecap. You can use the side of your hand or a soft mallet. Watch your leg jump when you find the reflex. Now switch roles.

12. **A second pair of eyes.** Using eye makeup, "paint" eyes on your child's eyelids so that your child's eyes will look open, even when they're closed! (This project was born of a desperate attempt in college to appear to be awake during a lecture.) Be sure to take

photos—your child will love seeing the developed pictures. In the meantime, make up your own eyes so kids can see what it looks like. You'll hear squeals of delight.

 13. **Prepare an emergency kit.** Where I live, kids are required to leave an earthquake kit at school, filled with enough food and clothing to last a day, in case disaster strikes and they can't be immediately rescued. Whether your area is prone to earthquakes, tornadoes, floods, or fires, it's a good idea to have an emergency kit handy. Make one, including candles and matches, a flashlight, solar blanket, can opener, toy, small cans of juice and meat or tuna, other snacks, a change of clothes, and first-aid items. At the end of the school year, if kids haven't had to use their kits, they celebrate by gobbling up the goodies inside.

14. **Illustrate a riddle.** Draw a picture that captures your favorite riddle. Older kids can compile a joke book.

15. **As the world turns.** Using a globe (or basketball) and a flashlight, you can teach kids about the Earth's rotation. Go into a darkened room and have your child shine the light on the globe. As you slowly turn the globe, kids will see how the light, which stays in one place like the sun, gradually brings daytime to different regions. Make sure to point out that when we have nighttime,

people on the other side of the planet are in daylight.

16. **Make tracks.** Trace each of your child's feet on three sheets of paper and cut them out. You'll end up with six separate footprints—three left ones and three right ones. Now ask your child to make a trail of footprints. Young kids have a hard time arranging the feet correctly but will enjoy trying, and they love to see silhouettes of their own feet. Older kids can place the feet in a wacky arrangement and then try to step on each one without falling over.

17. **Learn about roots.** Go outside and pull a weed to show kids its roots. Plants use their roots to drink nutrients from the soil. Try to find a tree whose roots extend several yards beyond the trunk. Tell kids that roots also anchor a plant to the ground, prevent erosion, and are so strong they can break cement and crack walls.

You can also demonstrate the way plants drink indoors, by putting carnations or a stalk of celery in a vase of colored water. Watch as the color appears in the petals or travels up the veins of the celery stalk.

 18. **Solve a giant puzzle.** Using a poster board or a large sheet of butcher paper, help your child draw a large mural. Now cut it into large puzzle shapes and mix them up. It's fun for kids to work

with such big pieces and finish such a "huge" project.

19. **Mathmallows!** Mathmallows are greeted by cheers and whistles in our family. Using marshmallows, we solve simple math problems. Give your child a pile of 10 marshmallows, then have him pull aside 6, to see what 10 minus 6 is, and so on. (I don't have to tell you what to do with the materials when you're finished.)

20. **Fill in the blanks.** Tell your child a story, but leave out the nouns. For example, "There was once a gigantic _____. It lived with a _____ that was tinier than a _____. They lived in a _____. Well, one day there was a knock at the door, and when they opened it, there was a _____," and so on. Older children can fill in missing adverbs and adjectives.

21. **Draw a blueprint of your home.** Using pencils and paper, sketch a floor plan. Small kids may want to walk miniature figures through the design. Older kids may want to design their dream house.

22. **Back words.** Spell words backward and see if they make new words. Some fun words are stop, tar, and pin. What would your name sound like backward? Think of some palindromes, words that spell the same thing forward as backward: (pop, bob, level, wow, and mom).

23. **Learn about primary and secondary colors.** Combine colored paints (or water tinted with food coloring). Learn how to get secondary colors from primary ones. You can create purple, orange, and green by mixing red, yellow, and blue. Make a color wheel if you like. Older kids can try to match paint chips or swatches of fabric by mixing paints to exactly the right hue.

24. **It's a leaf's life.** Now that autumn has arrived, pantomime what happens to a leaf: Let your child unfold, grow, change color, fall, rustle among other leaves, be raked up. Older kids could compose poetry or music that evokes these same images.

25. **Make up a story.** Look at a magazine picture and ask your child to make up a short story about what is happening in the picture.

26. **Tough choices.** Just as you played "What If" for safety, now play it for ethics. What if you spilled paint and the teacher blamed another child for it? What if a boy accidentally put his toy in *your* backpack, thinking it was his? What if the clerk gave you back too much change? What if the teacher lost the tests and asked each child to report the score he had gotten? What if you saw the answers to a quiz on the teacher's desk during recess? What if a book club mailed you more books than you had paid for?

You might tell your child that integrity is the way you would behave if you knew you would never be found out. And Confucius taught that while honesty is being truthful with others, integrity is being truthful with yourself.

27. **Make a mask.** Color or paint a face mask on heavy paper, then cut out the mask. Cut eyeholes, too. Now glue a popsicle stick behind the chin of the mask, so that the child can easily hold his mask in front of his face. Make several masks, if you wish. Role play. Let the child see himself in the mirror.

28. **Get the whole picture.** On a chalkboard or a sheet of paper, draw half a picture and ask your child to finish the other half. Begin by drawing half a circle and ask your child to finish it. Next draw a heart or a square. Try harder pictures such as a rocket or clowns. Much older kids can fold a magazine page so that only half is facing them, then slide a paper under the page and try to complete the rest of the picture. This is tough to do!

29. **Discuss opposites.** Find something tall and something short, dirty and clean, open and closed. Look for items that are old, new,

big, small. Older kids can think of opposites for harder words. funny, interesting, generous, adventurous, industrious, colorful and surprising.

30. **Watch your steps.** Count how many steps it takes you to go from here to there. This helps kids learn both counting and measuring. Stand in one place and guess how many steps it will take to get to another part of the room. (No fair leaping or taking baby steps, just to make your guess correct.) Now pick a new spot and guess how many steps to that one.

31. **Study volume.** Place a full bucket of water in a nine-by-thirteen-inch pan. Now immerse a toy in the water, and explain that you're about to measure its volume, or how much space it takes up. (Don't submerge your hand, or you'll end up measuring its volume.) Now see how much water overflowed into the pan, pour it into a measuring cup and measure the toy's volume. Try other toys, too—which has greater volume, the dinosaur or the truck?

1. **Make book covers.** Using brown paper bags, or any other large sheets of paper, cover some books and let your child decorate them with stickers or drawings. Preschoolers feel grown up when one of their storybooks is wrapped this way. And let's not forget their function—covers really do protect your books from wear and tear.

2. **Memorize a poem.** Select a nursery rhyme or short poem that's geared to your child's age and interests, and have her memorize it. Funny poems are often popular; a favorite of my children's is an anonymous one, which goes, "I'd love to be a centipede at Christmas; think how fun/To have a hundred stockings, instead of only one!" Memorizing verse is great mental exercise—try it.

3. **Make a water xylophone.** Fill a row of glasses with various amounts of water, then tap the glasses with a spoon. Can your child arrange them in the order of a scale? Can you play any songs

on your new instrument? A fun variation is to use food coloring to make the water in each glass a different hue.

4. **Sculpt clay letters.** This will help younger kids to review the alphabet. Sculpt objects that begin with each letter of the alphabet (apple, ball, candle, and so on).

5. **Learn a new word.** Have your kids use the word in three sentences.

6. **Show how a flame needs oxygen.** Light a short candle in a jar, then cover the jar. Have your child watch as the flame is slowly extinguished. If you have a fireplace, light a small fire and show how fanning the flames or using a bellows intensifies the blaze. Point out that a fire needs oxygen; that's why the best way to put out flames if you ever catch fire is to suffocate them by the "stop-drop-and-roll" method.

7. **Learn first-aid.** Get out your first-aid kit (or put one together if you don't already have one). Be sure it includes bandages, first-aid tape, scissors, first-aid cream, antiseptic wipes, a first-aid book, cotton swabs, tweezers, several gauze and cotton pads. Show your child how to put ice on burns and bumps, press on a cut to stop the bleeding, and bandage wounds with sterile gauze. If your child is young, you may

need to explain that certain items may only be handled by grown-ups.

8. **Can you describe it?** Have your child reach into a box without looking and feel various items you put there (or have your child stash the items in the bag for you to guess). Let your child *describe* each item he feels while he tries to guess what each thing is. Some good objects to include are: sandpaper, cotton, a feather, a marble, some plastic bubble packing, a prickly piece of fruit, a spongy eraser, and a rubber band. This game is bound to increase kids' vocabularies.

9. **Learn inches and feet.** With a tape measure, measure things in the house. Older kids can use the metric system.

10. **Make butter.** First, pour a cup of whipping cream into a clean jar and screw the lid on tightly. Now shake and shake and shake! This project cannot be completed in five minutes, but you can still give it a good start. (To be honest, I can never shake the jar long enough and I always end up beating the cream with an electric mixer.) After you've whipped the cream until the butter has separated from the liquid (which you may save or throw away), put all the butter chunks into a separate bowl. You may want to salt the butter a little, then spread it on bread, and sample it!

11. **Prove that the Earth is round.** To demonstrate why Columbus suspected that the earth was round, slowly move a tiny boat or toy along the surface of a ball or orange. Start from the back, and head over the top, toward your child's eyes. Tell your child to hold her fingers like a frame, and peep through them to see that the object becomes larger as it gets closer. But what tells you the surface is *round,* is this: Not only does the boat get larger, but you first see the top sails of the boat, then more of the sails, and finally the bow. If it were moving along a flat surface, you'd see the entire boat all at once, and it would simply get larger.

12. **Match quantities to numerals.** Draw a different number of dots on several three-by-five cards. (Dot stickers are available, too.) For little tykes, keep the numbers under ten. Now, on separate three-by-five cards, write out the numerals. See if your child can match the dot cards with the corresponding numeral cards. Older kids can match the dot cards to cards with equations such as 11 minus 6, or 20 divided by 4.

13. **Pretend to be travelers from space.** Land your spaceship on various countries on Earth and demand to be taken to each region's ruler. Find out who governs each country. Consult an encyclopedia or library book, if you need to. Pretend to let that

person decide your fate. You'll have fun finding out which countries have presidents, prime ministers, queens, and so on.

14. **Have you ever seen the wind?** Sprinkle a small amount of talcum powder on a hot light bulb, then watch as the powder rises, riding on a current of warm air. Tell your child that this is how air reacts to the Earth when the sun heats our planet. As warm air rises, cooler, heavier air rushes in to take its place. *Voilà*—wind!

15. **A tasteful experiment.** Look into a mirror, and stick out your tongue. Can you see the taste buds? Explain to your child that different parts of the tongue taste different things. For example, the back tastes bitter things, the tip tastes sweet things, the sides taste salty things. Experiment in the kitchen, by dipping cotton swabs into vinegar, salt water, and sugar water, and touching them to different areas of your tongue.

16. **Look at yourself in a spoon.** This will teach kids about convex and concave surfaces. Watch what happens to your image when you look at your reflection in both sides of a spoon. Kids will be amazed to see upside-down images of themselves on the concave side. Older kids can learn that while the eye may see something upside down, the brain turns it around to help us recognize what it is.

17. **Search for letters.** Using a newspaper, ask some kids to underline every *a* and *t* in purple. With red, circle every *o* and *r*. Put a green box around every *e* and *s*. This not only helps children recognize letters, but gives them practice in following very specific instructions. (Many kids cross out something when the teacher has asked them to circle it.) Older kids can hunt for words or pairs of letters such as *th* or *pr*.

18. **Let the music move you.** Play three or four short songs, and talk about the *feelings* each song evoked. "That one made me feel happy and excited, just like marching around the room." "That one made me miss Grandpa." "That one reminded me of the windy day when we went kite-flying." "That one made me feel dreamy and sleepy." What people do the songs bring to mind? What places?

19. **Play "In the Olden Days."** Like it or not, your kids think you grew up in the olden days. And after this project, you may agree with them!

Have your kids try to guess things that didn't exist when you were little. Some ideas: microwave ovens, videocassette recorders, aerobics classes, music videos, personal computers, current rock bands, disposable diapers, certain TV shows, and so on.

Now you can tell them some of the things that were part of the culture: fast food (remember the prices?) television, Silly Putty, skateboards, miniskirts, Dumbo and Pinocchio movies, a rock band named the Beatles.

20. **Create letter apples.** Ahead of time, cut some leaves from green construction paper and draw a tree with red apples. On each apple, print an uppercase letter, and print the same ones in lowercase on the leaves. Today, let your child glue the leaves onto the corresponding apples, to match upper and lowercase. Older kids can have riddles on the apples, and the answers on the leaves.

21. **Match shapes.** Draw simple shapes on a sheet of paper: circle, square, triangle, oval. Let your child look through a magazine and find similar shapes. Let him cut them out and paste them onto the proper shapes on the paper. For older kids, draw more complex shapes, or write out words such as "dog," "car," and "shoe" and have your kids find those items and glue them into place.

22. **Tell a funny story in a round.** Create a silly story by taking turns adding a sentence. My kids were laughing so hard when we

did this, they could barely speak. Each tried to turn our story's hero into a naughty boy who threw a cake into the face of a queen. When my turn would come, I'd have the queen open her mouth to swallow it whole, or step aside as the cake whizzed by. Finally Richie said, "And then he threw another cake at the queen, only he didn't miss, she didn't swallow it, she didn't use it as a facial, and she hated it." They both squealed with delight at having finally gotten around all my escape plans.

23. **Invent new exercises.** Kids are incredibly imaginative when it comes to finding new ways to do push-ups, aerobic workouts, and muscle stretches. (Some of their exercises can be pretty tough, too!)

 Today begins an eight-day series that leads up to Halloween.

24. **Paint a jack-o'-lantern face.** Paint a jack-o'-lantern on a paper plate. Hang it in your home to get into a Halloween mood.

25. **Work on your Halloween costume.** Try playing the part of your character as you put together your costume. If you're not making a

costume, or there's no preparation necessary, your child can still put hers on and perform a short skit.

26. **What's the difference?** Beforehand, make 10 drawings of different pumpkins. (Vary their size, color, and shape.)

As you show your child each drawing, ask her to say what makes this pumpkin different or special. For older kids, make the differences so slight that they really have to study them. This enhances kids' powers of observation and attention to detail and will help them with school-work involving similar skills.

27. **Sweet addition.** A sweet way to learn addition is to use Halloween candies. Three candies plus two candies equal five candies, and so on. You can gear this to older kids by using multiplication and division.

28. **Make witch's brew.** For this you'll need a little planning. Purchase some dry ice the day before. (Many supermarkets can get it, or check your phone book for ice dealers. A 10-pound block will only keep for 24 hours.) Pour orange soda into a "black cauldron" (or cooking pot). Drop in chunks of the dry ice and

watch as eerie "smoke" pours over the sides. Explain that dry ice is not made of water, but of carbon dioxide. *Be sure to warn your child not to touch dry ice, because it is so cold it can burn!*

 29. **Make tarantula cupcakes.** This is easy and wonderfully ghoulish. First, make or buy cupcakes ahead of time. Any kind will do. (We like to tint a white-cake batter orange, using concentrated coloring that professional bakers use. You'd have to use so much liquid food coloring the recipe would be thrown off.)

In the morning, turn the cupcakes upside down to form the bodies of the tarantulas. Frost the cupcakes with chocolate frosting (or better yet, tint white frosting black using a professional coloring). Now decorate the tops with red cinnamon candies, M&Ms, or gumdrops to create scary faces. For the spiders' eight legs, insert long strands of smooth black licorice into the base of the cupcakes.

30. **Discuss trick-or-treat manners.** You can practice Halloween manners by having your child ring an imaginary doorbell, while you open the door. Remind your child to say thank you, not

to ask for extras, and not to say they don't like something given to them.

This is also a good time to discuss Halloween safety, especially the importance of allowing you to check the goodies before kids eat any. Throw out any candy that isn't wrapped or is homemade by people you don't know. Talk about safe ways to walk through the neighborhood at night: wearing light colors, carrying a flashlight, and sticking with a group. Help your child to know the best action to take if other kids decide to vandalize or play a mean trick.

31. **Tell a scary story.** Make up one or get one from the library. Have your kids shout "Boo!" whenever you say the word "ghost," "cat," or "witch." An alternative to this game is to have the kids shout the letter *t* (or any other letter you've agreed upon) when they hear a word that begins with it. For example, "Once long ago, lived a boy named Timmy." ("*T!*") He had a pet tiger ("*T!*") with a long, striped tail. ("*T!*").

This concludes the Halloween series.

1. **Make an autumn scene.** Gather autumn leaves this morning, or beforehand. Sketch a bare tree trunk and branches on a sheet of paper. Now glue the leaves to the bare branches. Glue some along the ground, too. You can quickly create a lovely scene.

2. **Follow the bouncing ball.** You'll need a pitcher of water, three teaspoons of vinegar, and two teaspoons of baking soda. Drop mothballs into the mixture and watch them float to the surface again. (Mothballs are toxic, so be especially sure to supervise this experiment and dispose of the materials carefully.) When bubbles attach to the mothballs, they lift them to the top. Then the bubbles pop, and the mothballs fall to the bottom again.

3. **Carve apple people.** You may need to do all the carving if your children are young, but they'll still be enthralled as they watch you and make suggestions.

Peel an apple using a paring knife. Carve a nose, chin, cheeks, eyes, and eyebrows. Let the apple sit in a dry place for a few days and watch as it shrivels into a wrinkled "old" face. (It may even resemble someone you know!) You can make dolls with carved apple heads, if you wish.

 4. **Make silhouettes of your child's profile.** In a darkened room, shine one lamp brightly on a wall. Tape a large sheet of white paper to the wall and place your child on a chair between the paper and the light. You may need to experiment with your lamp, to produce a sharp shadow. Lightly trace your child's silhouette in pencil. Most kids have a hard time sitting still enough, so bring extra patience to this project.

After you've finished your silhouette, use it as a pattern to cut out another version, this time on heavier, black paper. Next mount the black silhouette on a larger sheet of white poster-board, which you may then frame. (Cut duplicates for relatives.)

I mounted silhouettes of Richie and Brandon on a thick white watercolor paper, where I'd already created an impression of their hands. I did the silhouettes and hand prints in coordinating shades of blue and the result is an attractive keepsake of my boys when they were small.

5. **Study human anatomy.** With the help of a library book or encyclopedia, learn a little anatomy. Kids are fascinated by what's beneath their skin, and you can teach them the names of bones and the functions of several organs. Older kids can draw a torso with heart, lungs, and other organs.

6. **Learn about letter blends.** Ahead of time, take an empty egg carton and write a different, two-letter blend in the bottom of each "cup." Here are twelve suggestions: sl, pr, tr, ch, gr, pl, cr, st, fr, sh, fl, br. Now have your child shake a marble or a penny in the closed carton. When you open the carton, look to see where the marble landed. The child must now think of a word that begins with those letters.

7. **Pretend to be!** Encourage your child's imagination. Have him pretend to be: melting ice cream, a baby bird, a plate of spaghetti, falling rain, a washing machine, a flower growing, and a kite flying. Then let your child try to think of some difficult things for *you* to try to act like.

8. **Learn about nutrition.** Draw a pyramid like the new one adopted by the Agriculture

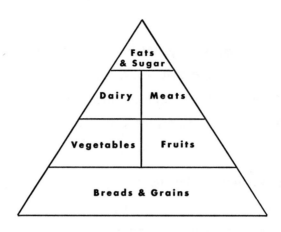

Department to replace the old "four basic food groups" chart. Divide it into *six* sections. Label the top section "Fats and Sugar" and explain that this is the smallest compartment, and that these foods should be eaten only sparingly. Divide the next level into two sections. Label the left one "Dairy" and the right one "Meats." We should eat moderately from these groups. The next level down, divided in two again, should be "Vegetables" on the left and "Fruits" on the right. The bottom level is largest, and should be labeled "Bread & Grains." It includes cereal, rice, and pasta. This is the group we should eat from the most.

Now have your child clip pictures of foods from magazines (or cut them out in advance). Ask your child to see if she can paste the items in their proper places in the pyramid.

Small kids have a hard time understanding why some foods belong where they do; this is a good way to get them thinking about what they eat. When this chart is completed, your child can use it to help you plan a dinner menu.

9. **Mirror each other's movements.** This project will get you both laughing. Play some music and stand facing each other. Start out slow, gradually lifting one arm. See if your child can copy you. Now switch turns and try to follow your child's movements.

10. **Start to needlepoint.** Buy a small square of loosely woven mesh or burlap and some yarn in a needlecraft or yarn store. Design your own pattern or buy an easy, pre-printed one. Using a blunt needle, show your child how to weave in and out of the holes to fill in the picture. This is great for fine motor coordination. And grandparents will appreciate the framed results!

11. **Learn about saving money.** If your kids don't receive an allowance, you may want to consider giving them a small one. Talk about why people save money, and some good reasons to save. Explain how a savings account at a bank works. Older kids can learn about budgets and figure out their own earnings and expenses. They can calculate how long it will take to save a certain amount.

You can also make a bank to help kids start saving. Cut a slot in the lid of a small box and tape it back on. Our kids use banks with dividers in them, so they can set aside money for different reasons: books, donations to church, toys, and college.

12. **Play "Hot and Cold."** Hide a thimble or any other small object somewhere in the room. (It must be in plain view, yet not obvious from a casual glance.) Now invite your child into the room, and as she walks around trying to find the thimble, tell her, "You're getting colder. Now you're getting hotter. You're boiling! You're frying!" and so on until she finds the object. Switch turns, as kids love to watch you search for something that they've hidden.

13. **Learn left and right.** Follow each other through the house, shouting, "Now turn left!" and "Now turn right!" You'll probably steer each other into walls, but that's half the fun. Older kids can be blindfolded, spun around, and then still try to guess which way the sofa is, or which way the front door is.

14. **Vote.** November is voting month. Talk about what voting means and how it works. You might create a family ballot to vote for some fun things: best bedtime story, favorite restaurant, best zoo animal, and so on. Tally the votes and teach the meaning of

majority rule: If the majority votes for chocolate cake for dessert, chocolate cake, it is. (But those who voted for ice cream may demand a recount!)

15. **Learn phone manners.** Practice answering the telephone politely. Even older kids can brush up on their telephone etiquette.

16. **Write invisible messages.** Dip a paintbrush or a toothpick into some lemon juice and write a secret message or draw a picture on white paper. Let it dry. Now hold the paper over a flame or a burner (don't let your child do this part) and watch as the secret message is revealed.

 17. **Make an unusual snack.** Some kids like these appetizers so much they'll ask for them for breakfast. Most grown-ups love them too, but can't guess what's in them.

They're deceptively simple to make: Wrap half a slice of bacon around a pitted date, and bake until the bacon is crisp. Serve them at parties, too!

18. **Learn about bar graphs.** Draw a large grid on a sheet of

paper, then hand your child several M&Ms. Ask him to count how many he has of each color. Along the bottom of the grid, color or write the colors of the M&Ms, even the ones he may not have. Going up the left side of the grid, write the numerals 1 to 10, one to a square. Now give your child crayons that match the colors of his M&Ms, and have him color in squares according to how many M&Ms he has in that color. Let's say the first column is for green ones and he has three greens. He'll color in three squares. If the next column is for brown candies, and he has five of them, he'll color in five squares, and so on. If you have any encyclopedias or books with bar graphs, show them to your child and explain that these work exactly the same way. When you're through, you can gobble up the materials!

19. **Trace your twin.** Use a large sheet of newsprint, packing paper, or wide butcher paper. Have your child lie down on it, and then trace around her with a dark marker. Let her color or paint it herself, including the outfit she has on today. Now cut out the life-size portrait and hang it on your child's bedroom wall! Extra ones can be folded and mailed to faraway relatives who won't believe how big your child has grown.

20. **Learn about archaeology and fossils.** Explain to your child that fossils are evidence of ancient life. Many fossils are imprints of organic matter that has been preserved in rock. If you have access to some real fossils, these are wonderful to study. If not, you can create a pretty good facsimile by putting some plaster into a cupcake holder. Next, have your child push a shell or other object into the plaster. First coat the object with petroleum jelly. (Plaster is easy to mix, but must be worked with quickly before it dries. You can also try using nondrying modeling clay.) After the plaster dries, pull the shell loose and examine the shape left behind.

21. **Break, crush, pulverize!** Kids rarely get a chance to utterly squash something with their parents' approval, but today that will actually be their goal. Put four or five crackers or a handful of cornflakes in a plastic bag, and let your child mash them with a rolling pin. As they are crushed he'll squeal with delight. The plastic bag will minimize the mess. You can save the crushed cornflakes or crackers and use them to coat chicken or make meat loaf. I like to use graham crackers because we enjoy pies that use graham-cracker crusts. I store the crumbs in the refrigerator until I'm ready to use them.

Begin a six-day series on Thanksgiving.

22. **Make a miniature Thanksgiving cornucopia.**

Use a sugar cone for the horn of plenty, and tiny foods or candies for the bounty that flows from it. Your harvest can include raisins, peas, berries, grapes, cereal, tiny fruit snacks, and other small edibles. This makes a pretty centerpiece, too.

23. **Act out "The Farmer and the Turkey."** To act out this skit, all you need is one hat (though you can prepare more elaborate costumes, if you wish). Here's how the play goes: A turkey enters, worried because a farmer is after him with an ax. He runs all around, looking for a disguise. Now the farmer enters but doesn't see the turkey. He says something about the turkey getting away from him every year, and resolves to catch him this year. Suddenly the turkey sees a hat on the ground and puts it on. Now he can strut right by the poor farmer, who is completely fooled, and even bid him good day. The turkey escapes and the farmer gives up. Hurray—the turkey got away again this year!

Let your child choose which role he wants to play, or do it twice, switching roles. You might want to make the rule that the farmer *must* be fooled by the turkey's disguise. (One of my kids grabbed me and said, "Aha—I've got you now!")

24. **Create a Thanksgiving turkey.** Trace your child's hand and have him cut it out. You can make a turkey from this. The thumb can be the head, and your child can color the fingers like feathers. Now add a face. Display your masterpiece!

25. **How do you spell "thanks"?** Write the word "Thanksgiving" vertically on a sheet of paper. Now, have your child name

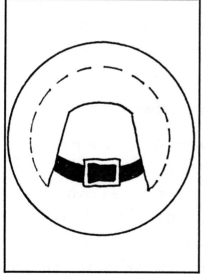

something she is thankful for, that starts with each letter in "Thanksgiving:" for example, Trees, Home, Animals, and so on. Help her write her words on the paper.

26. **Make Pilgrim hats.** Using safety scissors, cut around the inside of the rim of a paper plate, leaving a four-or-five-inch space uncut. (Save what you've cut for

the hat's brim.) Now, draw a rectangle which will become the top of a Pilgrim's hat. Your rectangle should touch the ends of the cutting lines. Now cut on the lines you just drew, still leaving the four-to five-inch space uncut. Fold the square up and draw a buckle on. This should fit most kids and makes a nice quick pilgrim!

27. **Have a corny Thanksgiving.** Thanksgiving is traditionally a time when we see lots of Indian corn, and corn in general. Europeans had never seen corn before the Native Americans introduced it to them and taught them how to grow it. Corn was one of the bountiful crops they celebrated at the first Thanksgiving feast (a three-day event). Fill a small jar with popcorn and have your kids guess how many kernels are in the jar. Count them. *My* guess is that you'll all be surprised.

This concludes the Thanksgiving series.

28. **Shop Smart.** Teach kids how to select the best produce in the supermarket. (My three-year-old became a more discriminating mushroom buyer than *I* was!) Using what you have on hand, show your child why you selected it and what you looked for. How should it feel? Appear? Smell? If you wish, prepare in advance by purchasing some examples of what *not* to buy, too. Give kids tips

about saving money, such as buying fruits and vegetables when they're in season.

29. **Make waves.** Fill a tall, clear jar halfway with water that you've tinted with blue food coloring. Fill it the rest of the way with salad oil, leaving no air space. Attach the lid and tip the jar sideways. You've just created a wave machine!

30. **Plan an adventure.** Modern explorers are excavating buried cities, diving deep into the ocean, visiting the Poles, and blasting into space. Where would your child most like to go? What would he find there? What would he need to take along? What are the possible dangers? What should he study in school to prepare for such a journey?

31. **Play catch.** Make this project more challenging for older kids by throwing a Frisbee or a ball of crumpled paper. Try throwing two things at once and catching them both. If you're right-handed, try catching with your left hand alone. You'll have fun and increase your other hand's coordination.

The holiday season can't come soon enough for me—I love everything about it. Every year I overdecorate, overbake, and overcelebrate. For that reason I've included a lot of holiday projects throughout the month. Most of these projects can be adapted into celebrations of the winter season. You can juggle these around, if you wish, doing some earlier or later than I've indicated. Do whatever works best for you and your family.

1. **Paint windows.** One of my kids' favorite holiday traditions is to get out the tempera paints, mix them with dishwashing liquid for easier cleanup, and adorn our windows with holiday pictures. Every year I paint a wreath with a little mouse asleep in it, and because I

once made the mouse a bit oversized, my kids insist upon an annual "Christmas Rat" painting.

2. **Make wrapping paper.** Here's how you do it: Cut several potatoes in half and carve into them Stars of David, angels, trees, menorahs, whatever you like. Do this part for young children. Be sure to wear smocks and spread out newspapers. Now let your child dip the potatoes into pie tins of poster paint, or use ink pads. Stamp the potatoes onto large sheets of tissue paper, newsprint, and even the long sheets of white paper you find in doctor's examining rooms! You can also create holiday cards with these potato stampers.

3. **Address an envelope.** Show kids all the aspects of addressing a card. Where do you write your own address? Where does the stamp go? What is a zip code? Older kids can learn postal rates, begin a stamp collection, or design their own envelopes. How about using sealing wax on your holiday greetings this year? Let your kids help you stuff envelopes and send out your seasonal wishes.

4. **Write a holiday letter.** Send a letter to Santa, or write a friendly letter to a relative. Older kids can compose a holiday or family song.

5. **Gifts from the heart.** Think of favors you will do for someone, resolve to break bad habits, or accomplish a goal. Write your "gifts" on heart-shaped cards, then punch a hole in the tops and hang them from your Christmas tree. Or, put them in a special box on the mantel, to be read on Christmas Eve.

6. **Talk about the past year.** Discuss happy events (such as a new pet or fun trip) that you experienced together. Some families may want to commemorate achievements by hanging awards, ribbons, and photographs on their tree or displaying them elsewhere in the home. This can help kids to emphasize the positive.

7. **Make a Star of David.** Draw a star with white glue on a sheet of waxed paper. You may want to place a pattern underneath, for your child to follow. Don't fill it in with glue; just leave it as an outline. Now sprinkle it with glitter. When it's dry, you can peel off the waxed paper, and hang it in a window!

 Begin a five-day gift-making series.

8. **Make a paperweight.** Glue scraps of cloth onto a smooth rock, then varnish or shellac it. You'll have a colorful paperweight. Older kids can paint a scene on a rock, using acrylic paints.

9. **Make a pillow.** Use fabric paints to draw a picture on a 12-inch square of muslin or linen. When the picture is dry, sew your painted square of fabric to another 12-inch square of the same fabric. Make sure the two right sides are facing one another. Leave unsewn three inches on one side. Now turn the pillow right-side out and stuff it with foam, cotton batting, (both are available at a fabric store), or use soft rags or pantyhose. Sew the pillow closed.

10. **Make another kind of paperweight.** Place some marbles in the lid of a jar. Let your child arrange them into a design. Now squirt white glue into the lid, so that the marbles are sitting in a shallow puddle of glue. In a day or two, the glue will harden and become mostly clear. If you like, glue trim or braiding around the side of the jar lid.

11. **Make a string holder.** You can make a very practical and pretty gift, using a can with a plastic lid (such as the kind cake frosting or coffee comes in). Punch a hole in the plastic lid, then thread the end of a ball of string through the hole, starting on the inside. Place the ball of string inside the can, and press the lid into place. Decorate the can with attractive adhesive shelf paper, wallpaper, gift wrap, paint, a collage, noodles glued onto paper and then wrapped around it, or whatever else your child chooses. You can also tuck a small pair of scissors inside the can with the ball of

string. Whoever receives this gift will always be able to locate string and quickly snip off the length she needs.

12. **Let it snow!** Children are fascinated by those globes that "snow" when shaken. Now they can make one for friends.

Here's how: Clean and dry an empty baby-food jar and lid, then on the *inside* of the lid, create a winter scene with miniature figures. Craft stores sell inexpensive miniature deer, trees, Santas, even tiny trains, and soldiers. You'll only need a few. Using waterproof glue, fasten your scene in place and let it dry. Later, fill the jar with water and add a pinch of white glitter. Put the lid on tightly and turn the jar upside down. When you shake it, "snow" will swirl around your winter wonderland.

This concludes the gift-making series.

13. **Wrap presents.** Cut pictures out of magazines and create a collage on a gift box. Another idea is to use fabric, aluminum foil, or wallpaper. Some of the new faux-marble papers can turn the box itself into a gift. You can let the gift dictate its own wrapping: Soaps and bath crystals can be wrapped in an embroidered hand towel. A pretty cloth diaper can cover a baby's toy; and dish towels are perfect wrappings for kitchen items.

When you add the bows or ribbons to your packages, try tying on a toy or a useful object, such as girls' barrettes or hair ribbons. A bundle of cinnamon sticks or sprigs of fragrant pine add warmth. Pine cones tied into clusters with florist's wire, then dusted with glitter are very festive. You can even make bows from matching wrapping paper. Don't forget to use the wrapping paper you made earlier this month!

14. **Make "finger" puppets.** Draw faces on your fingers and put on a puppet show. This discovery is fast and funny, and even if you can't wash off all the ink before the kids leave for school, they'll have a great reminder all day long of the fun they had that morning.

15. **Select a toy for the poor.** Instead of having Mom or Dad buy a new toy, let kids choose to give one of their own toys that's still in good condition. This is what we like to do because it involves kids more directly. Other families provide an entire Christmas for a needy family, including groceries, clothing, and other essentials.

Charities, churches, and hospitals can help you decide what's needed in your community or help you to place your gifts. This tradition of giving to the poor never fails to bring the real meaning of Christmas close to our hearts.

16. **Make soap crayons.** Your children will love bathtime with these wonderful creations, and they also make fun gifts. Mix one-eighth cup of water with seven-eighths cup of Ivory soap flakes. Mush and smush until it's fairly stiff and smooth. Now stir in 30 drops of food coloring until it's blended. Press the mixture into an ice-cube tray, candy mold, or solid-backed cookie cutter. Let the crayons dry for two days, then pop 'em out and suds up! You can color bathtubs, bodies, and tub toys with these washable crayons. Face painting is fun, too—just avoid getting the soap in your child's eyes.

17. **'Tis the season.** Today have your child make a seasonal picture using her favorite medium: the Nativity, or a happy Christmas, or Chanukah celebration.

A variation of this project is to sculpt holiday figures from clay.

18. **Add finishing touches to the Christmas tree.** Trimming a tree takes longer than five minutes, but placing the angel on top, or hanging one favorite ornament on a bough, can become a five-minute project. Try spreading the skirt underneath the tree, or placing the first presents there.

Those who don't celebrate Christmas can think of one quick task that will beautify the home: hanging a picture, adding a houseplant to a bare spot, putting fresh flowers in a vase, or polishing the menorah.

19. **It's for the birds.** Coat several pine cones with peanut butter, then roll them in seeds. (Birdseed is best, but any kind will do.) The seeds should stick well to the peanut butter. Now hang the pine cones outside, using string, and wait for the birds to enjoy this winter treat. Instead of pine cones, try hanging doughnuts outside on a string. Talk to your child about respect for living things.

20. **Talk about the miracle of prayer.** Teach your child how to pray and discuss things to pray for.

How about a prayer of thanks without asking for anything? If prayer isn't part of your household, talk about the importance of hope, how to make the world a better place, and so on. Discuss why these issues come up during the holiday season.

 21. **Make a calendar.** Get ready for the new year by making a calendar. Use a ruler to box off the days and months and be sure to illustrate. Talk about time and the year. Does your child know the order of the months? How many days are in a year? Why we have leap year? Explain what B.C. and A.D. mean.

22. **Find the starch.** This is a fun science experiment and easy to do. Simply drop iodine on various foods. If the drop turns black, the foods contain starch. Try a potato slice, cracker, orange section, cheese, slice of bread, celery, whatever you wish.

 23. **Make peanut or cashew butter.** Grind up about a pound of shelled nuts in a food processor or blender. Add a tablespoon or two of cooking oil. You'll get about one cup of nut butter. Be sure to refrigerate the results. Unusual nut butters make great gifts.

24. **Learn about disabilities.** Have your child wear a blindfold and earplugs for a few minutes, then talk about what it would be like to be blind or deaf. Tell the story of Helen Keller's struggle to

overcome her disabilities. Try having your child imagine having some other challenges such as dyslexia or brain damage.

You can also discuss your own handicaps and limitations—such as fears or phobias, insecurity, or even disabling allergies. Ask your children which handicaps people must learn to accept and compensate for. Are there any handicaps that people bring on themselves and can overcome with some effort? Talk about loving all people.

25. **Show how water clings (or just enjoy Christmas!).**
Something tells me you'll have a giant project already planned for today. But here's a science principle to learn. Place a cookie sheet on a puddle of water. Try to lift the cookie sheet. It's harder than you think because water really clings! This also explains why wet hair takes a long time to dry. Wet sand also shows cohesion.

26. **String a Kwanzaa necklace.** Kwanzaa is a seven-day African-American harvest festival that begins on December 26. Seven candles are lighted—one each night. They symbolize unity, self-determination, collective work and responsibility, cooperative economics, purpose, creativity, and faith. On the last day is a community feast including gifts, songs, and homemade necklaces. Your child can paint maca-

roni shells the traditional colors of red, green and black, then string them into a necklace.

27. Spin a dreidl. Cut a four-sided section from a cardboard egg

carton and draw the Hebrew symbols, Nun (‫נ‬), Gimel(‫ג‬), Hay(‫ה‬), and Shin(‫ש‬) on its sides. Push a sharpened pencil into and through the bottom, leaving the blunt end extended for twirling. Cut out and glue a flat cover for the open end, made of paper. Now your top is ready to spin!

28. Study tempo, rhythm, and pitch. Play some music and increase or slow down its tempo. (You can show the same principle by singing or humming a tune.) Now help your child clap out the song's rhythm or march to the beat. Next work on pitch by playing or humming one note, then another. Can your child tell you if the second note is higher or lower than the first note?

29. Play "Guess my number." Write a number between 1 and 20 on a slip of paper, and don't reveal it to your child. (For older kids, choose a number between 1 and 100.) Now have your child guess what it is in as few guesses as possible. You can help him narrow it down.

Let's say you're working in the 1 to 20 range, and you pick 17. Your child's first guess is 10. You say, "No, but the number is between 10 and 20." His next guess is 18. You narrow it down further, saying, "It's between 10 and 18." He guesses 15. You say, "It's between 15 and 18." Now he says 17, and you say, "Right! That only took four guesses!" A variation of this game is to play it with the alphabet. It's a good game to play in the car, too.

30. **Make a list of New Year's Resolutions.**

31. **Make some predictions for next year.** Save your forecasts and bring them out one year from today, to see who was best at predicting the future. Older kids may want to predict political, sports, or celebrity events. The best predictions are family-centered, such as "I predict our baby will be a girl," or "I predict Jimmy will learn to ride a bike next summer," or "I predict we'll get peaches on that new tree." How about, "I predict we'll have a wonderful year!"

HOLIDAY BONUS

Build a gingerbread house. This is much easier than you think, if you use graham crackers for your gingerbread squares. Spread out newspapers and have a box of graham crackers and plenty of decorative candies handy. Brightly colored gumdrops, jellybeans and M&Ms look wonderful, as do tiny candy canes and cinnamon candies.

You'll also need some white frosting to serve as glue and to give your house a snowy exterior. Here's how to make this cement-like frosting: Beat two egg whites with one-half teaspoon cream of tartar. When egg whites become stiff, stir in two cups of powdered sugar until well blended. This frosting dries out easily, so keep it covered with a damp cloth until you're ready to use it.

To make the house, first cover a 12-inch square of cardboard with aluminum foil, then spread a snowy blanket of frosting on it so the ground will look white. You can build your house on that. Hold the crackers together in the shape of a house by gluing them to an empty milk carton or other box, cut to the desired height. Bend a small piece of cardboard in half to form a roof, and glue crackers onto that. Now your little architects can decorate their creation! Be sure to take pictures of the final product!

INDEX

ABOUT THE AUTHOR

Joni Hilton earned a Master of Fine Arts degree in Professional Writing from USC. She frequently writes about parenting for national magazines. She also writes screenplays and books, including the novels *As the Ward Turns; Dating: No Guts, No Glory;* and *Braces, Gym Suits and Early Morning Seminary: A Youthquake Survival Manual.*

She hosted her own daily TV talk show in Los Angeles for four years, and is also a former news anchor. She was Miss California and a finalist in the Miss USA–Universe Pageant.

Joni and her husband, TV personality Bob Hilton, live in California with their children, Richie, Brandon, Cassidy, and Nicole.